START AND RUN
YOUR
OWN SHOP

MORE RELATED TITLES

Conducting Staff Appraisals

The secrets of successful press relations for the small business

'Not all books live up to their promises. This one does. ...a bargain.'
— British Journal of Administrative Management

Getting Free Publicity

The secrets of successful press relations for the small business

'A small but perfectly formed 'how to' aimed at small businesses with not much spare cash to throw around. ...consider this text your new best friend!' — www.thinkpinkinc.co.uk

Starting Your Own Business

Bestselling guide to planning and building a successful enterprise

'...full of practical hints about handling tax, approaching potential funders and finding suitable premises.' — The Independent

Understanding Financial Accounts

*Understand the principles and practice of accounting –
from book-keeping to VAT*

'Gives you the skills needed to make sense of financial information without assuming a degree in accountancy.' — Bookseller Buyers Guide

START AND RUN

YOUR OWN SHOP

How to open a successful
retail business

VAL CLARK

howtobooks

Published by How To Books Ltd
3 Newtec Place, Magdalen Road
Oxford OX4 1RE, United Kingdom
Tel: (01865) 793806. Fax: (01865) 248780
email: info@howtobooks.co.uk
www.howtobooks.co.uk

British Library Cataloguing in Publication Data
A catalogue record for this book is available from the British
Library

Cover design by Baseline Arts Ltd, Oxford
Illustrations by Nicki Averill
Produced for How To Books by Deer Park Productions,
Tavistock
Typeset by Pantek Arts Ltd, Maidstone, Kent
Printed and bound by Cromwell Press Ltd, Trowbrige, Wiltshire

NOTE: The material contained in this book is set out in good
faith for general guidance and no liability can be accepted for
loss or expense incurred as a result of relying in particular
circumstances on statements made in this book. Laws and
regulations are complex and liable to change, and readers
should check the current positions with the relevant
authorities before making personal arrangements.

Contents

Acknowledgements

Firstly I would like to thank Nikki Read of How To Books for giving me the opportunity to become a published writer and Melanie Jarman, my editor for helping me create what I hope is an enjoyable read.

I would also like to thank Ted and Irene Boud and Natasha van Diggelen for all their reading, helpful comments and encouragement. But most of all, I want to thank Chris for his endless help and unfailing support with this book and every aspect of our lives.

Preface

This book is for everyone who wants to open a shop.

It is aimed at the aspiring retailer with limited means but is also essential reading for existing retailers who are working too hard, not achieving their goals, and who want to expand or develop their business to move on. Wholesalers, sales reps and agents can also improve their businesses by learning about the reality of retail.

In 2003, a survey by *Woman & Home* magazine said that 34% of its readers want to start their own business.

A survey in May 2003 by Business Link, the government agency, found that:

- People take eight years to decide to become self-employed.
- Four out of five dream of doing something different.
- One in three specifically dream of setting up their own business.

For many, self-employment means opening a shop. It is a realistic and achievable action because it needs:

- no specific training;
- no compulsory qualifications;
- no huge outlay of capital.

In other words, it is an opportunity open to everyone. As Napoleon said, we are a nation of shopkeepers. It is a quintessentially British aspiration.

There is a current fascination with developing property for a profit. Yet with the average cost of a house being over £125,000 it is out of the reach of many people. A few thousand pounds – the cost of a small car loan – can set you up in business with a shop or market stall.

In 1996 I took £6,000 of a redundancy payment and opened a New Age gift shop in a small shopping development in an English seaside town. I quickly outgrew that space and six months later opened a second shop selling ethnic and alternative clothing and accessories.

Businesses can survive, thrive or fail. Some survive but little more. They tend to bypass the second stage, ending in the third – failure – usually within 18 months to two years.

There are 16 units in the development where I opened my shops, and over the last seven years I have observed 39 different businesses trade there. Some were there before I opened and continue to thrive, but 22 have failed.

When I opened in business I wished there was a book called *How To Do Everything*. I learnt through trial and error, feeling my way and learning both from my mistakes and those of others. This book speeds up the process, aiming for profit from day one. With a few basic guidelines, and nothing to do with luck, you can increase the chances not just of surviving, but of thriving in the retail world. What appears to be a very small shop in an average location can yield life-changing profits.

Use this book to open a shop in a reasonable location, with a five-year business plan, to:

◆ set up;
◆ grow;
◆ expand the business.

You will be able to increase sales, take on staff to decrease your workload, and at the end of five years you will have a set of books such that you can either continue to run the business, expand, or sell for a profit.

1

SETTING UP

WHAT SORT OF BUSINESS AM I GOING TO HAVE?

There are many questions to ask yourself when you decide to set up a business. These will range from 'Why am I going into business and what do I want to achieve from it?' to 'How will my business operate?' The answers to the first question may be very complex and personal to you but the second question is answered in this chapter:

The legal classifications of a business
Sole trader
You are on your own, no one to answer to, no one to tell you what to do – you are your own boss. You will, however, be responsible for purchases, sales, advertising and marketing, accounting, shopfitting, cleaning …

Partnership

◆ TIP ◆

If there is someone in your life whom you trust and respect, you may prefer to share the responsibilities – but also the profits.

It is good to have someone to share the burden of work and to throw ideas around with. This helps to keep you focused and stops you taking the business off at a tangent. Beware, however: you need to be sure that your objectives and those of your partner(s) are the same. Be quite clear about the allocation of work, how much each has invested financially and how the profits will be split. Unless these matters are clear from the start, there will be arguments about who is pulling their weight and who is not, who has put the most into the business in terms of time effort and money.

The other problem with a partnership is ending it. If you are undertaking a specific venture for a set length of time, that should be fine. If it is to be an ongoing venture, then when and how will you arrange to go your separate ways? Anyone who has ever been divorced will tell you that when a marital partnership breaks up the main asset usually has to be sold to give each party their share. In a divorce this will be the family home, but for a business … the business will be the main asset.

A limited company
This is a legal and regulated entity, which should give you personal protection financially if the business fails. It does involve extra administration and costs, both in setting up and ongoing.

If this is the option you prefer seek free advice from your local Business Link (see 'Useful contacts' page 199) and then from your accountant and/or legal advisor.

HOW DO I WANT TO TRADE AND WHERE FROM?

If you are a plumber or electrician selling a service, you can probably work from home, storing your equipment in the garage and using a desk in the corner of the lounge as your office. If you plan to sell goods, you will have a supply of stock, which must be stored and possibly displayed somewhere, and you will need someway by which your customers can obtain these goods from you. How you do this will determine whether or not you need premises to operate your business from.

Party plan

You take your products to your customers so do not need premises. Small items work well, such as jewellery, cosmetics and the original party plan classic – Tupperware. Certainly in the early days of your business, stock can be stored in a corner of your home with paperwork being done at the kitchen table.

Going into people's homes in the evenings or offices at lunchtimes to sell to them in their own environments is a cheap way to set up a business. This way of selling relies very much on the personality of the seller and would suit someone who is gregarious and outgoing.

Mail order

To do this really well, traditionally you would have needed to produce a glossy, colour catalogue, showing photographs of all the products you sold. This was a costly exercise to produce and frustratingly inflexible to maintain when you wanted to include new products or delete those that were no longer available. Postage was expensive to send copies out to all enquirers, not all of whom would have placed an order.

Nowadays, with the invention of the digital camera and the Internet, this is a much more appealing way to trade. There is no question that a professionally photographed catalogue should look superb but you can get started by taking photographs yourself and invest in the services of a professional when you are more established, with a better knowledge of what items will be regular sellers.

◆ TIP ◆

With a web-based catalogue it is possible to change the contents of the pages as often as you want.

A one-page flyer can be sent to prospective customers, directing them to your web site for the full catalogue.

Mail order can be run as a business in itself or as part of any other retail business. It may start from home and expand to an industrial unit on a business park, or operate from the stockroom of the shop or indoor market stall. If you manufacture your products or can source them at suitably low prices, you can even supply on a wholesale basis to other retailers.

Fêtes, fairs, festivals or markets

This can be a cheap and flexible way to start up. It provides market research on what sells best whilst earning the capital to set up a permanent business should you decide to do so at a later date.

Some events provide everything you need but for others you will need a decorator's paste-up table and a cloth to cover it, or even your own market stall. These, together with your stock, can all be stored in your own garage, garden shed, or rented lock-up garage.

You need to be strong and hardy to work this way. Setting up a market stall and carrying all the stock from your car to your pitch is hard work, especially if it is pouring with rain or worse, snowing. Some trading days will be a complete washout when trading in the open air.

Shops

Shops can be set up from scratch or taken on as a going concern by buying an established business.

A moderate investment is required for setting up from scratch, together with the need to research thoroughly both the market and the proposed location. You start with a blank canvas but can create a lasting and growing empire to be proud of.

Buying an established retail business is the most expensive option but it benefits from the security and goodwill of an existing client base and an established location. The risks of an all-new venture are reduced, as you have access to the business' accounts and can judge whether fresh impetus will even improve takings.

For more information about these two options see 'Buying an existing business v setting up from scratch', page 20.

FUNDING PREMISES

Premises are a substantial cost when setting up. As a new business, unable to provide references from your (business) bank manager and a commercial (not residential) landlord, you will be required to pay:

- three months' rent in advance;
- six months' rent as a deposit.

A 250 sq ft shop in a reasonable, secondary location could cost £10,000 plus VAT per annum in rent. This could mean paying nearly £9,000 to the landlord alone before redecorating, fitting out the shop or buying stock to sell, let alone getting to the stage of opening the doors to customers and earning any money.

> **◆ EXPERIENCE ◆**
>
> I was fortunate to set up in business during the recession of the early 1990s. There were many empty shops in the town and my landlord was anxious to find tenants. I was able to negotiate a rent free period and there was no suggestion of paying a deposit. As a result, I had been trading for two months and earned the rent before I had to pay the landlord a penny.

WHAT IS YOUR USP?

USP stands for Unique Selling Point. It is what makes you and your business different from the competition. Why will customers buy from you and not someone else?

Will it be because you offer:

- better service;
- greater convenience;

- faster delivery service;
- a better after-sales service;
- a wider range of products;
- car parking;
- child-care facilities;
- or has your product got a story to it?

Small shops can compete with the big boys because of their uniqueness and diversity. Independent stereo and television shops sell the same products as the likes of Dixons and Comet, but by offering a delivery or installation service they will be particularly attractive to the shopper who does not have a car or is technologically challenged. That is the story that will attract the older shopper.

◆ TIP ◆

Small businesses can be much more on the edge and up to the minute than large stores, getting involved with trends at a much earlier stage.

◆ EXPERIENCE ◆

I had been selling combat trousers for two years before they started appearing in shops like Marks & Spencer or even New Look. Once they were on the High Street combat trousers quickly became over-trendy and largely died out as a fashion item. Incidentally, I bought only combats from that supplier, until they suddenly brought out a range of Tommy Hilfigger fleece tops. These proved to be tremendously popular for a few months and then that trend died completely. I would never have become involved with selling them had it not been for the combats.

FINDING YOUR MARKET

The following are examples of what some people have found customers want to buy in their particular area:

- Imitation perfumes for £2.99 a bottle from a car boot sale near a council estate. This worked because although the people there did not have much money to spend, they were prepared to treat themselves once a week.

- An Internet café thrives in a town where there is a base of foreigners who want to keep in touch with home, for example a barrack town used by the Gurkhas.
- Fish and chip shops often rely on those leaving the pubs after last orders but one located by a market, opening early to cater for stall holders, can afford to close early. Much more sociable working hours for the owners and staff, and they avoid the hassles and dangers of drunk, and sometimes disorderly, customers.
- A seaside town increases its population dramatically during the summer months and gives its traders a new set of customers each week.

Competition comes directly from other shops selling the same products as yours, and indirectly from other ways that customers spend their money.

◆ EXPERIENCE ◆

In 1999 mobile phones really took off with every teenager having one. Girls' spending habits changed from using all their pocket money to buy nail varnish, to buying top-ups for their phones. Initially my takings took a dive but I retaliated by selling funky mobile phone holders and cases.

RESEARCHING YOUR AREA

1. Consulting the census

Your local library will have a copy of the latest census. From this, and your own knowledge of the area, you can compare different areas to find out about the ages and relative wealth of the people living there.

◆ EXAMPLE ◆

In 1996 I made a comparison between West Sussex, Great Britain as a whole, and my personal knowledge of the town I lived in. The 1991 census showed:

- **Home ownership**
  Great Britain   66%
  West Sussex   75.5% (above average. A fairly wealthy middle class
                     area perhaps?)
  Personal view   Appears to be quite high. Not many council estates but a lot
                     of bed-sit type rental accommodation in the town centre.

▶

◆ **EXAMPLE** *(contd)* ◆

◆ **Economically active** (% unemployed)

Great Britain	9.3%
West Sussex	6% (lower than average. Surprising as this is a rural county with few industrial areas.)
Personal view	Unemployment seemed to be quite high. Also lots of young mothers pushing pushchairs around town all day – good customers.

◆ **% of Retirement age**

Great Britain	21.2%
West Sussex	26.5% (above average. The retired are not great spenders when it comes to shopping.)
Personal view	Very high numbers of retired people.

◆ **Conclusion**

West Sussex was where I lived. It was too far to commute to another county every day so I would have to think of something that the people of West Sussex would want (and need) to buy from me. Was my idea of a New Age gift shop the right one? More research required.

---

2. Assessing the pros and cons in your area

The marketing term for this is a SWOT Analysis.

This stands for: Strengths;
                    Weaknesses;
                    Opportunities;
                    Threats.

The purpose of the analysis is to examine your intended project and pick holes in it. Think of all the reasons why your idea will work in your intended location; and then all the reasons it will not.

◆ EXAMPLE ◆

This was my analysis for a New Age gift shop in an arcade of shops in a small, coastal town in West Sussex:

	PROS	CONS
PEOPLE	I have experience of running a business.	Who will cover if I am ill?
	I have qualifications and experience in management and accounting.	I am new to the town and do not have local family or friends to help out.
	I am fit and healthy.	
	I do not need to take a wage initially as I have savings to support me for the first three months.	
	I have the skills and tools to do my own shop fitting.	
PLACE	Lots of chimney pots.	High population of retired people.
	Several schools in the town.	Will there be enough trade in winter?
	University campus in town centre.	Shop quite small; will I quickly outgrow it?
	Tourist trade in summer.	Do locals shop in town or go to the larger, trendier town nearby?
	Strong pedestrian flow.	
	On route from car park to main shops.	
	On route from beach to main shops	
	Like-minded businesses around eg music shop.	
	'Essential ' businesses around eg lunchtime sandwich bars.	

▶

◆ **EXAMPLE** *(contd)* ◆

PRODUCT	No direct competition in town. Selling consumable items eg candles (repeat sales).	Is New Age too trendy? Is there a lack of product familiarity?
	Regular sales eg greetings cards.	
	Stock will be trendy and can adapt to changes in taste.	
	Goods will be bought for self as well as for presents.	
	Stock will be bought on 30 days credit.	
	All sales will be over the counter (no bad debts).	
PROMOTION	Stock will appeal to a young market (kids tell their friends).	
	Prices range from 'pocket money' to expensive.	
Conclusion:	There are a lot more positive than negative points. This idea should be looked into further!	

FINDING YOUR LOCATION

Where do you want to be in business? Could it be where you live? Your local shops may not always seem the most obvious location but consider:

◆ A long journey to work every day takes up valuable time. Especially in the early days, when you will need to be in the shop early and stay late. An hour each way in the car could have been the day's bookwork and orders done.

If your home town is a holiday resort:

- Will the local population provide sufficient trade to keep you going out of season?
- Could you afford to close?
- Would your lease allow you to close?
- Could you use the quiet part of the year constructively, say to travel abroad sourcing and importing stock?

Think about where you go to shop: for your groceries, clothes, household goods, furniture and furnishings, presents, sports kit, and so on. Ask your local family and friends where they prefer to go. If none of you shop locally for one specific type of goods there could be a gap in the market and the need for that type of shop in the town. If everybody you know prefers to travel for all of their shopping needs, your local High Street could be in need of more regeneration than you will be able to give it single-handedly by opening a shop there.

What am I selling and to whom? Am I a specialist, niche market, mostly mail order or do I need high volumes of sales?

The parade of shops at the end of the street could provide:

- low rental;
- customer parking;
- easy access;
- street frontage;
- back-room workshop or storage facilities to a business that does not rely mainly on passers by, impulse sales or high volume trading.

This would be:

Good for a specialist antique clock repairer advertised in *Yellow Pages*, the horological magazines and on the Internet, distributing spare parts by mail order, with a workshop in the back room and parking outside for customers to deliver and collect repair items.

Bad for fashion jewellery, greetings cards or other goods where a busy location is needed to give high volumes of passing trade, often buying on impulse.

RESEARCHING YOUR CHOSEN LOCATION

1. Count the chimney pots

Every business benefits from high volumes of customers and the denser the local population (I am talking quantity here not IQ) the greater the number of potential customers. If you have enough people, all you have to do is stock what they want. The perfect product at the best price can only be a best seller if there are sufficient people to buy it.

2. Who and what is round about

♦ Is your intended site near 'like-minded' shops? If you are a florist, can you find a location near an undertaker, a bridal wear supplier or outside the bus/train station to catch people on their way home from work?

♦ Are you in a busy thoroughfare with lots of people walking past? The more exposure your shop has, the more likely you are to make sales.

♦ Where is the nearest car park? Parking, particularly if free, brings people into the town and is important if selling bulky items that customers need to collect.

♦ If your product is aimed at young people or 'clubbers', how many schools, colleges or nightclubs are there in the area?

♦ If the target customer is retired, are there many bungalows or retirement homes nearby?

> ♦ TIP ♦
>
> The saying is 'location, location, location' – the three most important points to consider when setting up a business.

3. Counting the footfall to find the most customers

Once you decide on a location, the local council may be able to provide information on pedestrian footfall ie, identifying different streets in a town by the number of people who walk through them to discover the busiest areas. There are market research companies that will sell you this information but you cannot beat checking for yourself.

Checking for yourself

Think of your local town centre:

- the shops on the top floor of the indoor shopping centre that are never as busy as those downstairs;
- the street that used to be so busy before the one-way system was brought in and now nobody walks down there or can park there;
- the number of times in the past five years that shop round the corner from the main precinct has changed hands … four, five, six? Make sure you are not number seven.

The best location for any shop looking for passing trade will be the one with the most passers-by and you will be looking to rent the best location you can afford. Shops are classed as being in:

- Primary Locations
    - the busiest part of the High Street
    - the main entrance to a busy shopping centre
    - the centre of things

- Secondary Locations
    - the quieter ends of the High Street
    - the approach roads to the main shopping area
    - not quite in the centre of things

Then there are others that I will put in a third group

- the 'Terminal' Location
    - the one where it is only a matter of time before the latest tenant goes out of business.

If the only shop to rent in the whole town is at the end of a no-through alleyway, with derelict and boarded up warehouses all around, don't kid yourself. Customers are not going to come flocking down there just to see what you sell. If the location is in any way quirky – upstairs, on its own, off the main drag – it will not be as profitable as the one 50 metres away that is in a secondary, but conventional location.

Generally a primary location will be too expensive for a small independent just starting out. In 1998 a 500 sq ft town centre location in Stevenage, Hertfordshire was to let for £100,000. With a six-month rent deposit and a quarter's rent in advance, this prices it out of most new retailers' reach.

Once you have found a location that interests you, it needs to be checked out for:

Footfall Stand outside and check how many people walk past. Do this on particular days of the week and at particular times. Compare this to other parts of the town on the same days and times.

> **◆ EXPERIENCE ◆**
>
> I compared a shop unit by the railway station on a main road with one in a covered arcade. My expectation was that there would be more people passing the unit by the station. The actual result was that far more people walked through the arcade.

The opinion of fellow traders

Whether you are planning to buy a business or take over vacant premises, speak to the other traders around and see if you can get a feel for what business is like in that area. Some may view you as competition and not tell the truth but if you speak to enough people you will be able to build up a reasonably accurate picture of the situation. If you are planning to take on premises in a communal development where you will share the same landlord, find out if there are any particular issues you would want to know about.

> **◆ EXPERIENCE ◆**
>
> I enquired about the landlord with one group of tenants and found that for some time not all tenants had been paying their service charges. As a result there were a number of serious maintenance issues with the property and existing tenants were being asked to contribute large lump sums of money to effect the repairs. I found out more information than the landlord had volunteered to me and was able to make a more informed decision on whether or not to take on the lease – I did.

Amenities

Is it opposite the busiest bus stop in town? If it is in an arcade, is it walk-through or dead-end? What is at either end? Where is the nearest competition? Will your neighbours complement or compete with what you are planning to sell?

◆ EXPERIENCE ◆

I opened my second shop, selling ethnic and alternative clothes, jewellery and accessories, opposite my first, a New Age gift shop. Next door there was a CD shop and an Extreme Sports shop, which made that part of town quite a centre to draw in young people. The street was a covered arcade, the main thoroughfare from the beach and the town's main car park, to the High Street and town centre bus stops.

Getting it wrong

Remember the boom time of the 1980s? A study was done to find a centre of mass affluence in South East England – a place where a shopping centre would be built that would be in the centre of what was deemed to be the wealthiest part of that area. The idea was to build a specialist shopping centre for small, exclusive, up-market shops that would be highly attractive to the surrounding high-income earners.

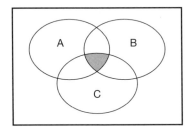

A, B and C represent areas in the South East of England, where people with high incomes had been identified as living. The hatched area represents the most central area for all of the above people to travel to. This was calculated to be the most favourable place to build the new shopping centre. The place chosen was Hatfield in Hertfordshire and the new building was called The Galleria.

Hatfield was hit badly by the recession of the late 1980s/early 1990s, losing the town's main employer – British Aerospace. The shop units in The Galleria failed to attract sufficient exclusive boutiques to fill the centre. Those that did sign up quickly closed down.

The shop units were too small to appeal to large high street multiple retailers such as Marks & Spencer or Woolworths. The centre limped along, half open, with falling visitor numbers and financial problems for those who owned/ran the building. It was eventually turned into a discount, outlet centre and seems to be surviving happily in that format – pretty much the opposite of what it was designed to be.

FINDING A PROPERTY

- Commercial property to let may be advertised in the local property paper, usually at the end of the residential lettings.
- Specialist trade magazines, such as *Dalton's Weekly*, advertise businesses that are being sold as going concerns.
- Commercial property agents and business transfer agents are listed in local telephone directories.
- Contact your local authority to see if they keep lists of property to let/for sale.
- There may be a to let or for sale board outside the shop itself.

THE FINANCIAL AND LEGAL ARRANGEMENTS OF TAKING ON PREMISES

In town centre retailing it is highly unusual (if not completely unheard of nowadays) for the retailer to own their own premises. Dedicated property management companies or investment companies such as pension schemes own most commercial property in desirable locations. These landlords will offer you either a licence or a lease to occupy their premises.

Taking on a lease

A lease is a legally binding document that entitles the tenant to trade at a specified address for a stated period of time. If you leave during that period of time, then you (the tenant) are still responsible for paying the rent. If you can find a new tenant, who is acceptable to the landlord, then you should be able to assign (hand over) the lease to the new tenant, who will take over paying the rent for the remaining period of the lease. Legally, however, you (the original tenant) are still liable should the new tenant, or any subsequent tenants, stop paying the rent. This is the standard type of agreement for renting a shop.

Taking on a licence

A licence is also a legal agreement, but one which can be terminated at any time by either the licensee or the landlord. This can be an advantage if your plans are short-term but it does not give you any long-term security. A licence will be issued for example:

◆ on a shop that is available only for a short period of time, eg if it is earmarked for re-development;
◆ for an indoor market stall, which is not a permanent trading location but the licence gives you the right to the same location on the market, each week of your licence;
◆ for most small storage units, such as lock-up garages.

Length of lease and rent reviews

Shop leases have traditionally been for 25 years or more but following the recession of the early 1990s, this has tended to be cut to shorter periods such as 12 or 15 years. You might even be lucky and agree one for six years.

The period of your lease will probably be split into three or five year periods, depending on the length of the lease. At the end of each of these periods you will be subjected to a rent review. Most leases specify an upward-only rent review, meaning that even if other rents in the area have fallen, yours will rise, or at best remain the same. If your landlord is pushing for a rent rise above inflation, it is worth employing the service of a commercial property surveyor, who will charge in the region of 10% of the finally agreed rent. (See also 'Renewing the lease', page 169.)

◆ EXPERIENCE ◆

At the end of my first lease, the landlord tried to push the rents up from £7,750 and £9,750 to £9,500 and £14,000 respectively. Having failed to negotiate a more reasonable figure myself, I employed a commercial property surveyor to negotiate on my behalf. The process took over 18 months, cost me £1,750, involved both shops being re-measured (one was found to be smaller than it had previously been!) and resulted in new rents being agreed at £8,000 and £10,250. These figures were less than the £8,500 and £10,500 I had originally offered to pay!

Rental charges

Rent is a complicated calculation. It is charged at so many pounds per square foot, but not every square foot of a shop is worth the same value. The front part of a shop, looking from the window inwards, is the most expensive part. The rent for a shop that is wide but not very deep, will cost more than the shop next door, which is narrow but goes back a long way.

If there is an upstairs sales area, the rental for this area will be less expensive than that downstairs.

The value per square foot varies depending on which part of the country and which town the shop is in. It will also vary depending on which part of town and the exact part of the street.

Premiums and other charges

A premium (or key money) is a sum of money charged by the previous tenant, payable by the new tenant for the right to take over an empty shop for the remainder of the lease. You get nothing more for your money than that. Premiums were routinely charged in the late 1980s when the economy was booming but fortunately, this practice does not seem to have been resurrected since and I am not aware that premiums are currently being charged.

Another practice that was commonplace in the boom-time of the late 1980s was the need for prospective tenants to make payments to property agents just to ensure that they were sent details of properties that were available to let. Those who were not in the know about this did not receive any mailings. I do not believe in subscribing to such practices but suspect that some agents (who have not sent me information on shops I know to be available) still operate in this way.

Rent deposits

Unless you have been in business before, prior to taking possession of the shop most landlords will require you to pay a rent deposit of six months' rent (plus VAT if the landlord is VAT registered) in addition to the first quarter's rent.

It is always worth trying to negotiate this amount downwards but unless a landlord is desperate to find new tenants (during a recession or if this particular shop unit is difficult to let) you are unlikely to find much leeway.

Legal costs

> **◆ TIP ◆**
>
> A licensed conveyancer specialises in the transfer of property, and will do the same job for you in taking on a straightforward lease as a solicitor, but will probably cost less.

> **◆ EXPERIENCE ◆**
>
> On the sale of two shops in 2003, a licensed conveyancer charged the seller a flat fee of £500, agreed up front. The buyer used a solicitor, did not agree a fee and was charged by the hour. The buyer's final bill was over £4,500.

Planning consent

For retail premises, categories include:

A1   General use;
A2   Financial and professional services;
A3   Food and drink.

Applications are normally acceptable for A1 usage but there may be a limit to the number of A2 and A3 premises that your local council will permit within a parade of shops.

Categories for industrial warehouse uses include:

B1   Light industrial use;
B2   General industrial use;
B8   Storage or distribution.

You will need to consult your local council about the planning consent for the shop you intend to take on but there should be no issue unless you are proposing a change of use. You will also need to consult them for planning permission if you intend to change the shop front or erect imposing signage.

Communal locations

If you are taking on a shop in an indoor market, arcade or small shopping centre, where you and your neighbours will share the same landlord, there may be restrictions on your intended usage. This should protect the interests of existing tenants and prevent a new tenant coming in and competing directly with the same products that are already being sold. Keep your usage broad to allow you flexibility but be specific about the lines that you want to protect.

BUYING AN EXISTING BUSINESS V SETTING UP FROM SCRATCH

When buying a business as a going concern you are buying:

◆ the goodwill;
◆ the existing customer base;

- the concept of the business;
- the owner's expertise.

You will agree and pay a price for all of this, as well as for the shop fixtures and fittings and the stock.

Some people will pay a lot of money for a business and change it substantially because they do not actually want that business, but buying it is the only way to be able to trade in that particular location. Others will buy a business that they plan to make major changes to because poor management has led to it performing at well below its potential.

Unless you have good reasons for making changes, such as the above, any business that you buy should continue to be run in the existing format and full advantage taken of the advice and guidance of the current owner. Otherwise, why are you buying the business? There would be less financial outlay in taking on an empty shop and setting up from scratch.

Buying an existing business

This will involve a high initial financial outlay but you will know from having examined the books what trade is being generated and how much can be predicted as an ongoing income. See page 182, for information on how to value a business. In the first weeks after taking over the business the established stock base need only be replenished until you have found your feet and are ready to tweak it.

In order to decide whether a business is worth buying, at the price being asked, the current owner will need to let you see the last three years' accounts. These will tell you:

- how profitable the business is (or at least how much is being declared to the tax man). You will want to see that there is a substantial amount of money left over for the owner after all the bills have been paid each year.
- what liabilities there are. In other words, what debts are owed by the business – and will you be taking these on if you buy the business?

◆ TIP ◆

Employ an accountant who specialises in small businesses to scrutinise the accounts and advise you accordingly.

If you do purchase the business, you will also need to:

◆ see a breakdown of each week's takings;
◆ find out which weeks of the year are exceptional (either up or down) and why;
◆ ask what normal stock levels are throughout the year;
◆ find out how much stock to order and how often;
◆ find out if it is necessary to build up extra stock levels for exceptional times of the year;
◆ get copies of all stock buying records;
◆ ask what additional staffing is required over busy periods eg school holidays;
◆ have it written into the contract that there be a proper hand-over period when the previous owners work alongside you and tell you all you need to know. This will depend on the complexity of the business and your previous knowledge but you should listen, ask questions, take notes and absorb as much information from the previous owners as possible; even the best of us can always learn something new.

◆ EXPERIENCE ◆

With well over 50 suppliers used on a regular basis and so many different stock lines held, I would recommend a month handover for a novice buying my business.

Setting up from scratch

Obviously none of the above information is available for a business that is not yet in existence. Your SWOT analysis, footfall investigations and other market research will be much more important to you than if you are buying a tried and tested going concern. *You* will be the one taking this research and testing it in the marketplace.

The big advantages in setting up from scratch are:

- The initial financial outlay will be much lower.
- You will be able to make your mark on the business from day one.
- There will not be any inherited 'baggage' from the previous owners (a history of bad practice which has sent customers elsewhere).

The downside (or perhaps the scary side) is that:

- The amount and regularity of initial income can only be guessed at.
- It can take time for customers to know you are in business and build repeat sales.
- All stock will be new to you. There will be no tried and tested sure-fire lines that you can rely on to provide a steady income.

Anyway, with your mind on that old proverb 'scared entrepreneur never earned her first million' (or something similar), you do have this book, which will lead you through the areas you need to address to set up a thriving business – starting with the business plan. A thorough business plan will help you to establish in your own mind why you are doing this and what you need to do to succeed. It will also provide you with credibility when you approach banks and other professional advisers.

WRITING A BUSINESS PLAN

Before you get to the stage of signing a lease, write a business plan. This needs to cover:

- Why you are going into the business.
- What your personal and business goals are.
- What you want to achieve from it.
- Why it is going to be a success.
- Why people are going to buy your products.
- Why your business will survive when so many others do not.

If you need to borrow money to set up the business you will have to write a very full and professionally presented business plan for the bank. This should include details of:

- the company structure – sole trader/partnership/limited company;
- what the business will do;
- the market size and potential;
- competitors;
- suppliers;
- cash flow forecasts;
- projections of takings and growth;
- a complete résumé of all the people involved;
- your qualifications, experience and the strengths you will bring to the proposed business;
- the proposed premises;
- any plant, machinery and vehicles;
- your assets and financial needs.

Be realistic

◆ TIP ◆

Calculate how much money you need to earn for the shop to break even and how much money you need to earn to live off. There is no point saying you can live for £50 a week when the mortgage on your house is £1,000 a month.

When writing the cash flow forecasts you will be able to enter accurate figures for the likes of rent and rates once you have found your proposed location, but will have to estimate how much you will be spending on telephone or stationery. Remember that the more your turnover goes up, the more you will spend on things like carrier bags and probably wages, but your heating and lighting costs for example will remain the same.

Turnover ratios are available for some types of business such as grocery and menswear shops. This means that if £x of stock is held in a shop floor area of y square feet, then turnover can be expected to be £z. For most types of business, however, you can only guess.

CHOOSING A NAME

This is the identity of your business. It needs to:

- stand out from your competitors;
- reflect the personality of the business;
- be memorable.

Think of any connotations, both positive and negative, and also of the type of graphics that can be used with the name to get your business noticed.

'Co-operative Funeral Directors' is tasteful and describes the business. 'Bodies Are Us' certainly describes the business but can only be described as offensive.

'Clippers' or 'Snips' are safe names for hairdressers. They would suit a barber where older men are the main clients. 'Expressions' or 'Images' would appeal more to women and younger men who want something more than a short back and sides. 'Greys' and 'Curl Up & Dye' are names I have actually seen for hairdressers but somehow they just put me off!

'Expressions Bridalwear' implies new, exciting and individual. 'Basket of Threads' paints a good picture for a needlework shop.

The name needs to reflect the personality of the business. 'Enchanted Sun' was the name of my first shop (a New Age gift shop). It encompassed the mythical aspects of the shop and was very in keeping with the dominant themes of the day. The name was a hit. When I first opened, I kept a dish of little sticky address labels on the counter so that customers could take my details away with them (these can be stuck straight into an address book or diary and kept, unlike a business card which is easily lost). The local school children kept coming in and taking them. This was very puzzling until I found out that the coolest thing was to have my shop details on your pencil case!

For 'Cave', my second shop (an ethnic and alternative clothes and accessories shop), I drew on images of Stone Age men and prehistoric animals for the graphics.

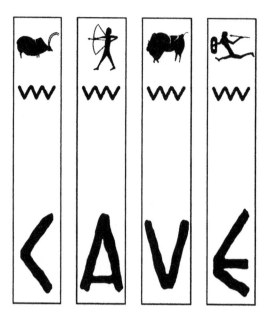

This logo looked great on carrier bags but customers seemed to be unable to read the font when it was used for sign writing the name onto the shop windows. Almost without exception, everyone thought it said 'sale' and that there was a permanent discount on prices!

Another problem I have encountered with that name is its lack of original-ity. There are other shops called 'Cave' that use the same suppliers I do and deliveries are often sent to the wrong shop.

Whatever you decide to call yourself, remember that people have an unfailing ability to find alternative ways to interpret what you thought was so clear.

◆ I always wonder at people advertising their business on the sides of their vans as 'Shoplifters' when I should be reading it as 'Shopfitters'.
◆ In North London there is the 'Theobrama Chocolate Shop' (meaning 'food of the gods' in Latin), which is frequently read in the Irish way as 'The O'brama Chocolate Shop', much to the annoyance of its owner.
◆ In the music world there was that 1970s hit song 'Sue Lawley' (the band Police, who sang it, thought the words were 'So Lonely') or that great old Christmas carol 'While Shepherds Wash Their Socks By Night'.

THE BUSINESS SIGN

The signs you have outside your shop need to attract passers-by to come in. They need to be:

◆ Clear and easy to read.
◆ Eye-catching. Remember that this effect will gradually wear off and for people who see the sign regularly, it will eventually fade into the background so it is necessary to change signs at suitable intervals.
◆ Compliant with your landlord's requirements, local council bylaws and both fire and health and safety regulations. It would be a shame to design and make a fantastic display only to be told to remove it.

Maintain your signs so that they do not become shabby looking or dangerous. They are your 'calling cards' on the world and first impressions count.

CHOOSING A COLOUR SCHEME

For the shop front

As with the name, the colour scheme needs to make a statement about the shop and what it sells but also needs to make it stand out from the others around.

I used a yellow/orange/red flame effect for the paintwork of 'Enchanted Sun', which stood out well between a conservative black gloss (very fitting for a jewellery shop) and a dark green (appropriate for a shop called 'The Woods'). 'Cave' is painted a deep purple, which is probably the colour most closely associated with ethnic and alternative fashion.

> ◆ TIP ◆
>
> Look at what is next door. If you are surrounded by bright and wacky colours and designs, then make your shop stand out by being more conservative – and vice versa.

For the inside

The colour scheme for the walls inside is a different matter. Whether you stock goods that are brightly coloured or very dark, you want to display them against a plain background and much as I hate to say it, magnolia paint is probably as good a choice as any.

FITTING OUT THE SHOP

Wall fittings and other shelving

Slat Wall is a display system using sheets of MDF, with horizontal grooves cut across the front of them, which are attached to the walls. Shelves, clothes hanging rails, glass display cabinets and so on can be hung from them and the heights easily adjusted. They come in a variety of colours or plain, which can be painted. I paint mine with Dylon clothes dye. This gives a subtle effect but gives me a wide choice of colours, which can be used to tie in with the shop's image.

If you can afford to fit out with Slat Wall straight away then do so. It is an expensive initial investment but gives flexibility for everything that you want to display in the shop.

Whether you use Slat Wall or freestanding shelves, you will need a range of shop fittings. These can be picked up second hand from:

◆ other shops closing down;
◆ small ads in the local paper;
◆ second-hand and junk shops.

Ikea is great for new glass cabinets and shelving at affordable prices.

Flooring

The main choices are stone or ceramic tiles, wood or a laminate, linoleum or carpet. The pros and cons are as follows:

◆ Tiles are long lasting, and easy to clean. It is a lengthy job to lay them. They can be noisy to walk on.
◆ Wood is very trendy but scratches and I would not want to own one should stiletto heels come back into fashion. Noise can be an issue.

- Lino style floors are to be expected in a supermarket but cheap and down market in most other shops.
- Carpets are quick and easy to lay. Cheap carpet will wear out quickly so it is worth spending more for industrial quality. Carpet tiles have the added advantage of being easy to move around, enabling worn or stained areas to be swapped or replaced individually. The downside is chewing gum, which is frequently trodden into my carpets and is difficult to remove.

The deciding factor for me is that things are always being dropped in a shop, whether by customers or staff. Carpet, being soft, means fewer breakages.

A classic mistake that new business owners make is to over-do the refitting of their premises. The ultimate in this is taking up a perfectly serviceable floor covering and replacing it with a carpet that has been specially woven to incorporate the name of the premises.

◆ EXPERIENCE ◆

One of my shops was fitted out with carpet tiles when I took it over. They did not fit to the wall, however, as they had been cut to go around previous shop fixtures. Did I put down a new carpet? Not when there was a supply of half-price carpet tiles to be had at the local DIY store. The new ones were brown; the original ones were blue – but who noticed!

Another carpet that I inherited when I took on a lease had been very worn where the previous counter had been. I moved the counter and these patches were exposed for all to see. Did I replace the carpet? Not likely. A subtle application of carpet tape kept the worn part in check as a temporary measure until the shop had earned enough to afford a new carpet.

Both the mismatched tiles and the tape were still in place when I sold the shops many years later. Had they affected sales in the meantime? Not in the least. Did they prevent the sale of the businesses? Clearly not!

Security
Think about security when laying out the shop.

◆ TIP ◆

Ideally you should be able to see every nook and cranny but in reality you cannot see through customers, so decide which areas are the priority.

Site the counter where you can stand and view as much of the shop as possible. Having it right next to the door may help to deter shoplifters but it is better to have it somewhere a little less obtrusive so that genuine customers are not put off from coming into the shop.

Leave plenty of space for access

Make sure there is room for customers to move freely around the shop. The gangway should be at least the width of a child's buggy. Customers will be put off coming in if the shop looks too crowded. This is less obvious on weekdays when it is quiet but most important on Saturdays when people have come out deliberately to spend their money.

You will probably lay the shop out several times over the first few months before you find one that suits best and will then start selling something large that requires a complete change about – but that's retailing.

SUNDRIES

Price labels, clothes hangers, paper bags and other sundries can be sourced locally through *Yellow Pages* or *The Trader*. If there are no local suppliers, then buy mail order from a company like Morplan (see 'Useful contacts' page 197).

There are a number of shop-fitting suppliers which you can visit in Commercial Road, in London's East End. This is a centre for the rag trade, with numerous clothing wholesalers supplying to small retailers and market traders.

And finally,

KEEPING COSTS DOWN

Keep your costs as low as possible when setting up to give your business every chance of success. You need to be ploughing your initial takings back into the business, expanding on your stock and introducing more expensive and unusual lines.

Cars and vans

Do not, particularly when you have just set up your business, blow your money on a new car – either bought or leased. Give your new business a car that is paid for rather than expecting the business to pay for one.

If you must buy a car there are some very good models, with less than 40,000 miles on the clock, for under £1,000. Have it serviced each year, check the oil regularly and such a car will be good for another 80,000 miles. This will do very well for your business, particularly if you are carrying stock around – it is an absolute waste to ruin a brand new car.

Beware of buying a van and putting your shop logo down the side, which will advertise to thieves what might be inside. Unless you need to deliver furniture or other such bulky items, there is no need to waste money in this way, whatever your accountant tells you.

Stationery packages

Forget it. They are a waste of money and of little benefit to you, particularly when you are starting out and need to spend money firstly on stock and secondly on display. Unless you are a limited company you do not need headed paper. Simply set up a master on the computer and print it as part of each letter you send. If you are VAT registered, remember to include your VAT number on all letterheads.

When going round trade shows, suppliers will ask for your business card but it is not necessary to go to the expense of having these printed – they are of no benefit to you. It is quick, easy and more cost-effective to write down your details or use sticky address labels (see Chapter 3, 'Making the sale').

2

BUYING STOCK IN THE UK

Having found the best possible location to sell from, the most important consideration is buying the stock – after all **it is** the business.

Stick a wad of cash in your pocket, have your shopping lists at the ready, and take your hatchback off to the West End of London to start buying. By the West End, I mean Acton, Park Royal and Wembley Stadium Business Park. Most major cities will have an area where there is a concentration of wholesalers (see *Yellow Pages* or drive around in your car) but unfortunately it is difficult to beat London as a centre for buying – I frequently meet traders from mainland Europe who drive over to choose their stock.

There are various ways to buy stock:

- by visiting a cash and carry wholesaler;
- at a trade show;
- from a sales rep or agent who will come to visit you;
- from a catalogue by phone, fax or on the internet;
- directly from abroad (see Chapter Eight).

BUYING FROM A CASH AND CARRY WAREHOUSE

Before visiting a wholesaler, carry out a detailed stock-check. Particularly for items like clothes, you do not want to guess and come back with exactly the same things you already have on the rail. Do not forget that the prices you see there will be exclusive of VAT (Value Added Tax, which currently adds a further 17.5% to the price).

◆ EXPERIENCE ◆

There is a large importer from India which is a very important supplier for me, selling incense, jewellery, bags and purses, smoking paraphernalia, feng shui animals, tarot cards and crystal balls, to name but a few. One of the many ranges I buy from them is carved wooden boxes. These are inlaid with brass shapes, such as a sun, moon, yin yang or elephant. There are innumerable shapes, sizes and designs but no catalogue. I find it difficult to remember exactly what I have in stock, which ones are selling best and those that are not good sellers. It is even difficult to write descriptions for them. The answer is to get one of each, lay them out and take a photograph with a digital camera. This can then be used as your master to stock-check against and take with you when you go to re-stock.

Advantages of visiting the wholesalers

- You can choose your colours and sizes. No risk of being given 'what is left'.
- There is usually a discount for paying cash and carrying the goods away.
- Immediate delivery. By taking the goods away with you, they can be on sale the next day as opposed to ordering by post, which can take a number of weeks to come through.
- You can ask for advice. Once you have used a supplier a few times, it will become clear which members of staff know their products and can be trusted to give advice on what is selling.

Talk to other buyers at the wholesalers. Find out what sort of shop they have, what they sell, where else they buy. Equally, some of the wholesalers are also retailers. Find out what else they stock, what associated products there are and what would be appropriate for your shop.

Cash and carry wholesalers are normally open Monday to Friday and for a short time on Sundays. They are always closed on Saturdays. Most will be closed on Christmas Eve and will not open again until January.

◆ EXPERIENCE ◆

It is a 100 mile drive to the Cash and Carry warehouses from where I live, which should take about two hours. I can leave home at 8 am, sit on the motorway and in the suburbs of London for hours on end or leave home at 6 am, arrive between 8 am and 8.30 am, and have a sit-down breakfast before my first port of call, which opens at 9.30 am. Whilst enjoying my first coffee of the day, I can use the time to go through the stock checks that I wrote the day before and note down exactly what I need to buy, or as quiet, creative thinking time.

Especially if you live in the provinces, going to visit the wholesalers in London can be a very long day. My *A to Z* is marked with places where I can park the car, get something to eat and use a toilet; examples being the big supermarkets and drive-in burger bars.

BUYING AT A TRADE SHOW

◆ EXPERIENCE ◆

The first time I went 'buying' at a trade show, I walked round, collected every brochure in sight, bought nothing and never looked at most of the brochures again – they sat in their carrier bags behind the sofa for years! I was too overawed by the amount of choice and had not prepared properly for what I really wanted to buy.

Take the following advice to avoid wasting your time and your household space.

There are trade shows held throughout the year, across the world. Important giftware shows are the Spring and Autumn Fairs held at the National Exhibition Centre (NEC), Birmingham in early February and September.

The Spring Fair is the biggest trade show in the world. It opens on the first Sunday of February each year and runs for five days. It is particularly important because it is the first chance for everyone to place orders for new stock after the Christmas rush and the January sales. Everything can be sourced there. It utilises the whole of the NEC with separate halls for general giftware, design-led gifts, cosmetics, greetings cards, art and framing equipment, household goods, luxury leather goods, Christmas decorations and jewellery from plastic beads to platinum and diamonds tiaras. There are also halls for wholesale buyers who are buying in very large volumes, including those who are prepared to deal directly with suppliers from the Far East, not all of whom speak English.

The Harrogate Gift Fair is held at locations throughout the town in July. It is smaller than the Spring Fair (as is the Autumn Fair) but is a really nice show to attend; you wander around the town going from the exhibition centre to various hotels to see different suppliers and most years can have lunch sitting out in the sunshine. It is also useful for placing early Christmas orders – your orders will take precedence over those of buyers who have waited until the Autumn Fair in September at the NEC.

PREPARING FOR A TRADE SHOW

Plan in advance to maximise your time.

Getting your ticket

Pre-registering for tickets saves time queuing to enter the show. This can be done on the internet or with the publicity literature that your suppliers will send.

Finding your suppliers

Prior to the Spring Fair, the organisers will send you 'The Little Black Book'. This lists all the exhibitors alphabetically and gives stand numbers.

Highlight suppliers you want to see, those you currently deal with and those you have dealt with in the past. Even if you do not intend to do an order it is worth looking at what they are selling, to get a feel for how trends have changed, what is new, and what has had its day. List names of suppliers you want to see but cannot find in 'The Little Black Book' – you may find them at the show listed under another name.

> ◆ TIP ◆
>
> Take a Dictaphone with you to make notes. Quicker and easier than writing, you can record reminders of the many diverse things you see – prices, quantities, location of suppliers, and so on.

Deciding how much to spend

Set a buying budget before going to the show. Allocate this roughly between each area of the shop, or the different categories of stock that you sell, depending on how you organise your business. List the types of stock you are in need of, such as:

- things to hang on the wall;
- items in the £2.99 or less selling bracket;
- a new cash and carry cosmetics supplier;
- 'stage setting' products which will give the shop that 'Wow' factor.

Allow plenty of time

Do not rush your visit. My buying needs cover giftware, jewellery, furniture, home furnishings, cosmetics, clothes and music. Ideally I spend a minimum of three days at the Spring Fair, visiting almost all of the exhibition halls.

Being comfortable

Many visitors get themselves all dolled up in their Sunday best, but what you look like will make little difference to the success of your business, except for your shoes. If your feet are tired and sore you will flag early. So whatever else you do, wear flat, comfortable shoes. To walk every aisle of every hall of the NEC is approximately 20 miles.

How to spend your time at the show

Start by walking around the halls, collecting catalogues and gaining information from suppliers. Unless you are very experienced, do not buy anything when you first see it. Buy the show catalogue at the end of the day so you are not carrying around a heavy weight.

If you are going to be there for at least two days (and I do recommend this), in the evening go through your notes and the catalogues you have collected to see whether your initial reaction was right. You will find yourself asking what you saw in some products. Discard these and make a list of all the people to go back to, the questions to ask and approximately how much you want to spend with each. After that, finish looking round and start to place your orders.

PLACING THE ORDERS

If it is a difficult order – something new, or that you are unsure about – make sure it is the first thing you do in the day whilst your mind is fresh and clear, so you can concentrate properly.

If you are only there for a day, sit down, have a coffee and go through everything carefully before placing the orders. A's candles may be cheaper than B's but you can buy more efficiently from C, who will supply both candles and wind chimes.

As you walk round, make notes of suppliers you have missed, those you need to go back to and those you have actually placed orders with. Over the following weeks and months check off what you receive against the orders you placed and chase those that are slow in arriving. It is amazing how many suppliers spend thousands of pounds on an exhibition stand but fail to send out the orders they take.

Finding out information from those on the stand

Try to speak to someone who has retail experience. Suppliers sometimes have their own customers working on the stand just for the show; some reps have run their own shops before 'going over to the other side'.

Whoever you speak to must be able to tell you:

◆ the prices;
◆ order quantities required;
◆ availability;
◆ the best sellers.

The best sellers

There is no point being told that everything sells well because there are always some items that sell faster than others. 80% of your sales will come from 20% of your stock so do not believe anyone who will only say, 'They all sell well'.

◆ TIP ◆

When buying a new range, ask the sales rep about any offers that are available. Often if you buy the full range of a specific product, you will be entitled to a free display stand, spinner or even a glass cabinet at a reduced cost.

How much to order

Look for companies where you can do small minimum orders, ideally no more than £200 carriage paid. The lower the price of the goods and the smaller the range of products, the lower this figure should be. Beware of companies where everything has to be bought by the dozen or more.

If you struggle to do an initial order, you will definitely struggle to re-order. Never buy anything because you are desperate to make up the numbers. If the item does not jump out and say, 'buy me', it will not speak to your customers either and you will end up selling it at a loss to get rid of it.

Delivery times

Check if goods are in stock and available for instant delivery.

Some wholesalers bring samples to the trade show, decide which lines have been popular, then fly out to the Far East to place orders with the manufacturers of those items. With a lead-time for the manufacture, six weeks' shipping from the Far East, an allowance for the clearing of customs, and finally unpacking the container at the wholesaler's warehouse, it will be at least three months before you receive your order.

Beware of companies operating from a non-UK address. Sometimes this is a speculative foray into the UK market. If sufficient orders are not taken, they may decide not to deliver. They do not tell you this and the money you have allocated for the order could have been spent on something else. This is why you should never pay at the time of ordering. Always wait for the pro forma invoice and details of delivery dates.

I have often found such companies incredibly slow to deliver. Either way, I could have spent the money on something else and made a profit before I hear from the non-UK supplier.

Finding a range

Look for a supplier that can supply you with a range of items. If you see one figurine that you like, you will need to like at least another two or three in the range to make an eye-catching display. One will look lost.

Spotting a trend

Before attending a show it is useful to check out your competition to see what they have in stock and what their customers are buying. Is something on the wane or on the up? Speak to your own customers and find out if there are things they want to buy that you do not have in stock. These are things that should be done on a regular basis throughout the year.

Once you arrive at a show, look out for stands that are busy, with plenty of people milling around, lots of staff writing out orders and other people clearly waiting to place orders.

In fashion, but should I buy it?

Just because there is a demand for it, is it something that will fit into your shop? Petrol sells in large quantities but would anyone think to go to a gift shop to buy a litre of petrol?

◆ EXPERIENCE ◆

Ty's Beanie Babies – small soft toys ('plush' to the trade) in the shape of various animals – were in huge demand around the time of the millennium. The trade stands were the size of a tennis court and you could not see the stock for the crowds of people, but there was nothing New Age about them and they would not have fitted into my shops, so I did not buy them.

Beware of getting onto the tail end of a craze or fad. In 1997 trade stands selling New Age music were really buzzing – the following year they were quiet. In 2000 it was balls of bath salts which fizzed up when dropped in the bath – but sales are now very flat.

If a product is on the trade stands of various wholesalers, but is something you sold several years ago and now no longer do, consider re-stocking it. Everything comes around again eventually and now may be the time.

Equally, if you have been selling something for several years, do not keep stocking it out of habit. If figures are down:

◆ relocate it;
◆ 'freshen' the display stand, perhaps with new designs of the same line;
◆ or get rid of it.

And while you are there ...

◆ Pick up some **trade magazines.**

Copies of various trade magazines are handed out free at the shows and this is an opportunity to read a different publication, to see if it is worth taking out a subscription.

The Trader, a monthly magazine full of advertisements for stock for small shop and market traders, contains even more adverts than usual during the giftware show months (February, July and September) and it is definitely worth picking up a copy. This is a useful magazine to use throughout the year when you are looking to source a new supplier.

♦ **Make a holiday of it.**

In retail you get little enough time off so make an event of your business trips and enjoy them. Accommodation guides can be obtained from the local tourist information offices.

NEC: when visiting Birmingham, I sometimes stay in Leamington Spa or Warwick, but generally opt for Stratford-upon-Avon. This is a very pictur-esque town with a wide choice of accommodation and restaurants and easy access to the exhibition centre.

There is a park by the river and in September, after a long day at the Autumn Fair, it is lovely to wander through whilst deciding where to eat that night. Stratford-upon-Avon has so many B&Bs that I never book ahead; just turn up in Evesham Place to see where the vacancies are. This is a short walk from the town centre where there are many wine bars and restaurants, particularly in Sheep Street. All can be recommended and a couple of favourites are Sorrento, an Italian restaurant in Ely Street and the Indian restaurant in Chapel Street.

Harrogate: when visiting the Harrogate Gift Fair it is vital to book accom-modation in advance if you want to stay in the town itself. Again there is an excellent choice of accommodation and places to eat.

London trade shows: I have found good value accommodation at the hotels in Sussex Gardens, just off Bayswater. The rooms are very small but perfectly functional and close to the underground station.

BUYING FROM A SALES REP OR AGENT

Your first contact with a company's sales rep or agent may be at a trade show or it may be when someone walks into your shop on the off chance that you will be interested in buying their products. Sometimes they are the owner of the business they are representing and may even be the person who makes the goods. Other times they are an employee of one company (a sales rep) or acting as an agent for many companies, with a briefcase full of literature about many often unrelated products. Some of these people will be very experienced and knowledgeable about their products, others will be full of enthusiasm for their new invention, and yet more will say anything in order to earn enough to pay the mortgage.

Beware of the ignorant sales rep, the one who does not know the prices, the stock, or which line is the best seller. They come into the shop with their fat briefcases and plonk themselves on the counter. They block access to you at the till so customers cannot pay. They block your view of the rest of the shop so you cannot keep an eye on shoplifters. They come in unannounced – one rep came in the week before Christmas, at lunchtime of all times, expecting to be seen. They stand in the middle of a busy shop shouting out wholesale prices in front of all the customers who hear these prices, see the products on the shelf, and wonder why you charge more than twice as much.

The bad sales rep will come in and do this with any member of staff: part-timers, Saturday staff, whoever is there. This could be someone who knows nothing about placing an order, is not authorised to do so and in most cases would be someone you do not share this sort of information with.

On the flip side, the good sales rep will arrange a time to meet with you prior to coming into the shop and will stick to that time, respecting the fact that your days are busy. The arranged time may well be before or after shop opening hours when you will have the time to look at products in depth and place a proper order, trying new products as well as replacing strong sellers. When meeting with you during shop opening hours such reps will be courteous to your customers, respect confidentiality regarding pricing and keep out of the way so that you can continue to run your business.

This rep will keeps records of what all their customers buy, and with this knowledge can advise on products that are selling well in shops similar to yours and so may be of interest to your customers. They will know which items sell well for everyone and will be honest about the occasional product that does not fly off the shelf. Price lists and order forms will be willingly provided so that you can place repeat orders between visits.

Do not be afraid to ask someone to leave and come back at a time that is more suitable. Be firm with someone who drags in a suitcase of samples and proceeds to spread them all over the floor. Tell them that you will be more able to spend money when you can spend time to look and choose. If they will not provide you with a copy of the price list think carefully about whether you really want, or need to, deal with them; all truly reputable companies will provide this information.

BUYING FROM A CATALOGUE

A catalogue is very useful because it allows you to see every product that is available, but if you can get a hard copy rather than just view it on the Internet it is also a useful place to record details of:

◆ which items sell well;
◆ what not to re-order;
◆ which colours and sizes are most popular;
◆ which items can be grouped together to make better displays and bigger sales, eg matching cushions, throws and curtains.

I place all my orders using a fax machine but they could be placed by email.

◆ TIP ◆

The important thing is to have a written copy of the order that is placed to prevent disputes about figures being misheard over the phone.

I prefer to write the order because then I know that nothing has been mistyped. It is also used to check off against the delivery note and invoice.

DECIDING WHAT TO BUY

There are various factors that will affect your decision to buy. These include

◆ rate of turnover;
◆ cost;

- usefulness;
- collectability;
- security and display;
- storage requirements;
- taste.

Rate of turnover

Consider your products in the following terms.

Division One

These are your consumable products, which you will sell year in and year out. Consumables are things that customers will use up and have to come back to buy more of. Examples include incense, candles, smoking papers, room fresheners and loo roll. In the case of incense, joss sticks have been selling since the 1960s and 40 years later sales are just as good as they ever were.

Division Two

Low priced, £0.99–£2.99 lines which need to sell in volume but will only have a limited life span. An example of this is key rings; one supplier produced a range of 366 key rings, one for each day of the year to cover everybody's birthday. After a couple of years, after large volumes had been sold, they were withdrawn and replaced with key rings featuring people's names – something else for the same people to collect or buy as a small present for their friends.

Each line will have a selling life of two to three years. The suppliers themselves will discontinue or change them, sometimes before you realise. Review sales figures annually. If sales have fallen, speak to your supplier about taking the stock back to change it for a newer line. Working in this way ensures that:

- the shop is regularly updated;
- stock keeps turning over;
- regular customers retain their interest in the shop.

Any sales rep worth dealing with will be prepared to discuss such an arrangement as it keeps their commission coming in.

Division Three

These are the specialist products. For a New Age gift shop, these are crystal wands, large crystal balls, chalices and other items that are not sold every day. For a sports shop, a running or rowing machine could be a Division Three product as opposed to training shoes, which are owned by nearly everyone. Sheet music will be a regular selling line for a music shop whereas large orchestral instruments will not be sold to everyone who comes into the shop.

Whatever type of shop you have, there will be Division Three products. Always ensure that the shop is stocked with a selection of these but be ruthless; if you find that your sales have dropped off from previous years then find a new line to stock and discontinue the previous ones.

Part of your Division Three lines will act as your shop dressing and provide centrepieces for your displays.

◆ **EXPERIENCE** ◆

The Harry Potter phenomenon has generated a great deal of interest in Wicca (witchcraft related products). I have been buying crystal 'magic' wands that are more expensive than the average products I stock. They are quite individual and are bought by a certain type of customer, so are not something I would expect to sell everyday. They do, however, enhance the display in the shop. They act as a centrepiece to displays of smaller crystal balls and tarot cards, which I do sell regularly. They help to focus people's attention, thereby helping the sales of cheaper, more general products. The bonus is that every now and then someone buys an expensive wand.

Some of these 'centrepiece' items you may buy once and never re-order, but it is like 'dressing' your house when you want to sell it – the extra outlay can be worth the expense.

Cost

Cost is probably the most important factor in deciding what to buy, particularly if you trade in a price sensitive area – and to be honest, where isn't?

◆ FACT ◆

The majority of people in this country are of limited means. Even those who would seem to have an enormous income usually have an enormous mortgage and school fees to match. As a result their disposable income may actually be less than people at the other end of the financial scale.

◆ FACT ◆

You are less likely to go wrong if you target customers at the bottom end of the scale financially, because then everyone can buy from you. If you only sell high price items and interest rates start to go up, or a recession takes a grip of the country, you will have fewer customers with money in their pockets to spend.

Imagine four shops. In good times all the shops do well, but in bad trading times, customers will scale back on their spending, especially for non-essential items.

Shop	Average Price	Boom Time	Recession
A (Exclusive)	£1000	Sales – Excellent	Sales – Down Drastically
B (Pricey)	£100	Sales – Excellent	Sales – Down
C (Affordable)	£10	Sales – Excellent	Sales – OK
D (Bargain)	£1	Sales – Excellent	Sales – Up

People who would have bought from the Exclusive Shop during good times will have less to spend when times are hard. They may not be able to buy from the Pricey Shop, but it is likely that they can buy from the Affordable and Bargain Shops.

When everyone spends less the Exclusive Shop may go out of business, but the Bargain Shop may do better than previous years because it will pick up a new group of customers. When times improve, the Bargain Shop can continue to benefit by increasing its range of higher-priced and better quality items whilst maintaining its range of low-priced, good-value items.

50p and £1 'swag shops' established a presence in the High Street in the recession of the early 1990s and have boomed ever since – they did not go out of fashion when the economy improved.

As you look for new products you will come across many things that are very nice and may well seem to fit in with what you sell, but some such items may be handmade in Europe and as a result will be higher priced than their Far Eastern competitors. If you are in a price sensitive area where your customers are reluctant to pay high prices, look for similar, cheaper products, probably made in China in bulk and brought into this country by the container load.

The selling price

Consider what price an item can be sold for. Not just the basic purchase price of the item but how much it is actually going to cost to put it into the shop to make it sell.

- Will the mark-up be 100% or does it need to be higher to cover heavy losses by theft/damage?
- Will it need to be sold in a box? For example, jewellery.
- Does it need any other enhancements? Pendants for example, sell better if they are on a chain.
- What about signage (the signs and labels giving product descriptions and prices)?
- Does it need special price labels?

A pendant, bought wholesale for £2, may be put on sale for £9.99 or more when extras are included. (Pricing is covered in greater detail in Chapter Three, page 65.)

Price breaks

There are crucial price breaks when selling. 99p is a throw-away amount, £2.99 is a pocket-money sale, and £19.99 is still a classic amount that people spend on a present.

Psychologically, handing over one bank note rather than two makes an item seem much cheaper. Items for £9.99 sell much faster than £11.99, but sales of £11.99 and £13.99 items are very similar even though there is still a £2 difference in price.

Usefulness

You know you have got this one wrong when your customers come to the counter and ask, 'What's this?' and whatever you reply they say, 'Yes, but what does it do?'

Glass vases that are not the right shape or size realistically to hold a bunch of flowers; china boxes or wooden bowls that indicate no obvious purpose; candle holders of a non-standard size – they might look pretty in their own right but they will not be good sellers. Not everything can be a good seller and there is (somewhere) a market for *objet d'art* but from experience I know only too well that if an item does not have an obvious purpose or a practical use, it does not sell. I might sell one or two but end up having to sell the bulk of them at a reduced price, usually making a loss overall.

Collectables

A collectable is something that people will buy across the whole range, not just one piece, eg Myth & Magic's resin Land of the Dragons figurines, or characters from children's film or television such as Disney or The Simpsons. Established ranges such as these are excellent sellers.

The Tudor Mint is a good example of a company that makes collectors pieces (the Myth & Magic pewter dragons and wizards, holding a crystal). Every year they discontinue a percentage of their figurines and bring out a selection of new pieces. Porcelain companies such as Royal Dalton, Coalport or Wade Ceramics with their decorative plates and figurines are very good at producing collectables, as are the top football league teams, each bringing out new team colours every year or so; obviously all their young fans want to wear the latest strips!

The following themes are also collectable and people will buy almost anything that incorporates their theme: pigs, penguins, cats (but not dogs), owls, sheep, cows, dragons, dolphins (although they are not as popular as they used to be).

A catalogue for your customers to view

If you have a supplier who produces a catalogue, keep a copy in the shop and let customers choose for themselves. This is particularly useful when the supplier's range is too big for you to stock all their products. Mark on it your selling prices and use it to take orders. Even if people do not actually place orders you will get feedback of what they like and can include such items in your regular orders.

Particularly in the quieter months of the year (January to March in the giftware trade), this personal contact helps to establish relationships with your customers.

◆ TIP ◆

A reputation for being helpful and willing to source unusual requests will keep people coming back to you, rather than your competitors.

Offer to order with no obligation to buy. Most people, once they have actually seen and touched the item, will buy it. If they do not then you will have an extra item to sell that you would not normally have bought. You may find that it becomes your new best seller or you may live to hate it! Statistically you should be quids in because I have always found that most people will buy the ordered item.

Security and display
Security for expensive and fragile items

There is no point in buying something if it is going to be stolen or broken before you cover your costs of buying it. If the item you want to buy is expensive or fragile consider how you will display it in the shop. Something that needs to be kept securely in a glass cabinet will sell more slowly than something that can be picked up, touched and brought to the counter by the customer. Such items are also more staff intensive to stock – a member of staff must leave the counter and go to unlock the cabinet for a prospective customer to examine the item. This distracts the staff member's attention from the rest of the shop, possibly allowing shoplifters to operate, and delaying other customers from being served. As a result, only expensive items really warrant the space and inconvenience of being behind glass.

Methods of display for fragile items

Items that are made of glass are particularly vulnerable to being broken in a shop, where people are carrying bags or wearing bulky jackets and moving around in quite a confined space. I have had problems with flower vases that are designed to stick to windows with suction cups (the suction is not strong enough to hold the weight for long), hanging crystals which people treat like wind chimes, thinking they will make a pleasant noise when knocked against each other (they don't, they only break), soapstone carvings that are top heavy or do not have flat bases and fall over if someone breathes too hard. Try and anticipate what display problems you might have before you buy something and think of ways to get round them.

Consider the amount of inconvenience in the shop if stock is constantly falling off its display. Think also of all those refunds you will have to pay out if people take something home and the item breaks as soon as it is used. Is it really worth stocking such items?

Storage requirements

Items that are fragile may be delivered to you in very large, well-padded boxes. You will need to store these to pack the goods in when you sell them. Have you got storage space?

One of my shops is very small, with no stock room. Some of the collectables come in boxes that are up to two foot cubed. Fortunately the ceiling of the shop is very high and I have installed shelves well above head height/useful selling height to store the boxes on. I attach string to the empty boxes so they can be pulled down, in a controlled fashion, using a long stick with a hook on the end. (Did I mention that you have to be resourceful to run a shop?)

Who you are buying for

If everything you have bought is to your personal taste, then you have not bought well. Remember that you are buying to sell, not buying to keep.

◆ TIP ◆

Your friends and family do not always like what you like and the general public certainly will not. Keep stock varied and cater for all.

When buying clothes in particular, I predominantly buy the colours I know sell best: lots of white, especially for blouses, blue in all shades, black, purples, an assortment of greens and pinks, and so on. Lastly, I will throw in a couple of 'rogue colours', eg orange or lime green because there is always someone out there who will buy them and variety makes the shop more interesting.

Listen to what your customers tell you. Particularly in the early days, it is very useful to keep a notebook of products that people ask for.

Never restrict your opportunity to make a sale. Women generally make many more purchases than men, but you should ensure that your shop does not deter men from coming in – their money is also legal tender!

Taste

Do not be frightened of the gross and offensive – it sells fantastically. I have sold inflatable sheep, chocolate willies, flying willies, chocolate boobs, jelly boobs, carvings of ethnic ugly men with obscenely large genitalia… The last one always sell much faster than those without! The less tasteful the better when it comes to a best seller.

HOW TO BUY

Budget

Set a budget for your general buying.

Your business plan shows an annual turnover of £150,000. Divide that by 52 weeks in the year to give an approximate weekly turnover of £3,000. Divide this by 2 (when marking up by 100%) and you will need £1,500 of stock coming into the shop every week.

Depending upon what type of business you have, this will increase in the run up to seasonal events, eg Christmas for giftware, Valentine's Day for florists, and so on.

Forward ordering

Clothing suppliers in particular expect orders to be placed a season ahead.

If you have to order in September for the following summer, and the weather turns out to be cold and wet, you will not want all the sleeveless tops and sun-dresses that you ordered so optimistically nine months before. As a small retailer, you are just not going to be able to sell that sort of stock; far better to be able to buy little and often from a cash and carry wholesaler so you can react to what is going on.

General v specialist suppliers

Try out new lines in small quantities from a general supplier to find out which ranges sell well for you, and then find a company that specialises in them. You can then expand the range and often obtain better prices.

How often to buy

Do not overbuy. The ideal system of ordering is just in time. Only order as much as you need; never hold excesses of stock and thus restrict cash flow. The danger, however, with just in time is that you end up with 'just too late' and you lose sales because you have not ordered enough stock.

Carriage-paid orders are usually £250 but some are as low as £50. Aim to hold approximately one month's stock from each supplier and eyeball the stock levels every week, placing orders accordingly. Trends change and particularly if you buy from a cash and carry it is better to go regularly (weekly if necessary) to see what is new. A particular design may be fashionable this month but out next month and if you have overbought you are not going to have the money to buy what is new.

Seasonal trading
Christmas
For businesses such as gift shops, this is a very important trading time with some shops doing a third of their annual turnover in the pre-Christmas period. It is the only time of year when large volumes of goods should be held. Spend the year finding what is a good seller and place orders at the July and September trade shows, so that the stock starts coming in as early as August.

Consider buying enough to last till the end of February. By having such quantities you will not run out before Christmas and regret not having bought enough. If you have bought badly you have a long run up to Christmas to get rid of it. As Christmas draws nearer the public get more desperate with their present buying so even if you have to reduce prices you should be rid of it all by Christmas Eve.

After Christmas
To go into January fully stocked helps ensure January's takings are higher than if you close the doors Christmas Eve desperately needing to place orders.

Most suppliers close until after the New Year and as this is school holiday time, with people having Christmas money to spend, you will be losing sales. A shop functions at its best when fully stocked and takings will be higher in years when you are better prepared and better stocked. Deliveries after Christmas are slow to come in as many lines are out of stock.

Other seasonal events
Valentine's Day and Mother's Day are to florists what Easter is to the chocolate shops. As a small gift shop, however, I am wary of such events.

Mother's Day is a welcome boost to trade in March and virtually anything with 'Mum' on will sell. I do not, however, buy items especially for other events such as Valentine's Day, Easter or Halloween; in my experience, they do not sell. At the end of November last year I walked past a shop window covered in flying witches. They may have been excellent sellers (positively flying off the shelves!) but it looked like a bulk-buy for Halloween that had not sold.

3

MAKING THE SALE

People often say, 'I could never be a good sales person, I am not pushy enough.' They are wrong, because a good sales person is never pushy. Making sales is about making the potential customer feel comfortable and relaxed, and avoiding saying or doing anything that will put them off. The basis of good selling is good communication – from the seller to the customer and from the customer to the seller.

COMMUNICATION

This is the transmission of a message, idea, view or attitude from one person to another. The success of any communication is dependant upon the information being sent clearly, and the person to whom it is being sent receiving and processing that information so that the message can be understood. Communication is fundamental to the running of a thriving business. It

- increases sales;
- ensures effective staff recruitment;
- decreases staff turnover;
- increases productivity and the effectiveness of both you and your staff.

Outgoing communication

This consists of:

- words spoken   (7% of the message)
- tone of voice used   (33%)
- body language shown   (55% or more).

Words

One word can have many different meanings. People say and use words in different ways. Out of context words and phrases have completely different meanings.

All these factors can make words confusing and so they need to be backed up with other information.

Tone

Think about the following sentence: 'I did not say you stole the money.' Now say it out loud, emphasising the highlighted word:

'*I* did not say you stole the money.'
'I did *not* say you stole the money.'
'I did not *say* you stole the money.'
'I did not say *you* stole the money.'
'I did not say you *stole* the money.'
'I did not say you stole the *money*.'

Your tone changes the meaning each time, even though it is the same sentence.

Body language

You arrive at work and see your boss with her hands on her hips and an angry expression on her face. Clearly she is angry but when you ask what is wrong she says, 'Nothing!'

You visit a friend and ask if he is busy. He replies, 'No, of course I've got time to talk to you.' After a few minutes you notice him looking at the clock and drumming his fingers on the arm of the chair.

Which do you believe – the words or the body language?

When people are in agreement with ideas and attitudes they copy each other's gestures. Next time you are in a pub or coffee shop watch how two people sitting together behave. If they are getting on well together they will lift up their glasses and drink at the same time. If one leans forward and rests their elbows on the table, the other will take up a similar stance. If one crosses their legs to the right the other will sit in a similar way. They will be maintaining eye contact, smiling and nodding as they talk.

For those who are not getting on together you will see them drink at separate times; one may have their legs crossed whilst the other has both feet on the floor; one is slumped in their chair whilst the other sits erect but angled away. Sometimes the gestures are aggressive with arms folded and a frowning expression. Eye contact is less and there is little if any feedback to whatever conversation is being made.

Improving communication through body language

It is possible to make somebody feel more at ease by 'mirroring' them – matching their body language.

Try sitting next to someone who is angry and defensive. Their arms and legs will be crossed. If you sit in the same manner, they will subconsciously feel more at ease with you than if you had sat in a relaxed pose. Without making any obvious gestures, mirror what they do. Partially unfold your arms and legs, leaving them crossed at the wrists and ankles. As the other person follows you, gradually uncross them completely.

This applies to all of their body language: posture, orientation, weight distribution, gestures, facial expressions and eye contact. Also their voice: volume, tone, pitch, tempo, sounds and breathing rate.

They should be unaware of what you are doing but if you have rapport you will be able to lead their behaviour and achieve mutually desired outcomes.

Incoming communication

This is not just hearing the words that are said. The words and their delivery need to be interpreted and compared with existing knowledge. Only then is it possible for you to plan your reaction and respond.

◆ TIP ◆

When the person you are communicating with fails to listen you feel frustrated, misunderstood and even angry.

Good communication

For this to happen, there needs to be a two-way process with both parties understanding the message.

From the transmitter:

◆ the words are clear and concise;
◆ the tone expresses the meaning;
◆ the body language confirms the message in an open and honest manner.

The receiver:

◆ listens;
◆ gives feedback;
◆ demonstrates understanding;
◆ feels comfortable and at ease.

With customers, this results in a sale. With staff, work is carried out efficiently and effectively.

Putting it into practice

However original we try to be, some situations will leave us speechless and it is useful to have a few 'scripts' to fall back on. Here are some of mine:

'Just looking'

Remember the last time you walked into a shop and the assistant asked, 'Can I help you?'

No matter how many times the question is asked, the answer will be the same: 'No.' OK, some people will throw in a 'Just looking,' or even a 'Thank you,' to be polite, but everyone seems to have an inbred fear of being asked a question. Customers say 'No' almost before you can finish speaking.

Far better to greet everyone coming through the door with a smile, make eye contact and say, 'Good morning'. Follow this with, 'Thank you' as they leave. Customers then realise that you are friendly to everyone, not just picking on the ones that look like a soft touch.

In a small shop with only you and one person browsing, the atmosphere can feel pressured so keep your eyes on them but carry on doing what you were doing before they came in. You can break the ice with a comment about the weather and follow it up a few minutes later, when the person is looking at something in a cabinet or up on the wall, with, 'They are lovely aren't they? Let me know if you would like a closer look'.

This is not a question, the person does not feel threatened, and the standard response is 'OK' or 'Thank you'. It may even open a conversation. By far the majority of people will then buy something, but if they do go away without buying at least they know you do not bite and they will come back.

'Is it all right to have a look round?'

Some people will peer round the door and ask, 'Is it all right to have a look round?' A good icebreaker here is to say, 'Of course! Come in! There's no charge for looking.'

Always try to make eye contact. You are aiming to build good rapport to make sales and as such your gaze should meet about 60% to 70% of the time during your conversation. When people are being dishonest their gaze will meet ours less than one third of this time; an important point when you are looking to distinguish genuine shoppers from shoplifters.

Show them what they really want

Listen to what the customer is saying. When people say, 'I want to buy a wind chime as a present for my sister', show them the wind chimes. If they are not paying attention to what you are showing them and start saying things like 'what lovely candles', 'that would look really nice in my room', and so on, do not persist with the wind chimes; show them the candles. That is where their focus is and you could end up selling both the candles and a windchime.

Do not pressurise

If the customer is dithering over a big purchase, do not push them. Take the sale away from them. Say, 'If you're not sure then leave it. Why not go and have a coffee and think about it? You can always come back for it later.'

This usually results in a sale; often immediately, sometimes after that coffee, and occasionally for a less expensive piece that better fits their budget. The important thing is that the person is not being put under pressure and so is unlikely to go home and have a change of mind.

Help the customer to choose

Try to establish at an early stage what the customer is after:

- Is it a present for someone else or for themselves?
- What size?
- How many?
- What do they want to use it for?
- How much are they prepared to pay?

Presents tend to have an upper price limit. It obviously varies depending on the age of the customer and their ability to pay, but in general terms £20 is not far from the norm for an adult friend or family member. Close family and partners command more, and if it is being bought for the person's own use then the sky can be the limit. This information is very important if you hold a range of the items that the person is looking for.

I stock clear crystal balls that some people would use for fortune telling, from 20 mm diameter to 150 mm, together with a variety of semi-precious and other coloured balls. Prices ranged from under £5 to well over £150.

Establish what the customer actually wants before showing every possible option. This prevents the customer being overwhelmed by choice and leaving without buying what they came in for. Showing the one that most closely fits the need and the next price up may result in a bigger sale than was originally intended.

Selling by the bundle

Laying out the shop with like products together helps to promote multiple purchases.

◆ TIP ◆

Relaxation music, next to aromatherapy oils, next to candles, helps people to envisage a relaxing evening in the bath with music playing, candlelight flickering and the sensuous smell of oils in the water.

When somebody comes to the counter with an oil vaporiser in hand, before you ring it into the till ask, 'Do you have oils and candles for that?' The answer will inevitably be 'No,' and you can show the customer what they need. Even if they do not buy at that point, they know what you stock and can return when they do have a need. It is important to ask 'Do you *have* oils and candles?' rather than 'Do you *need* ...?' The difference is subtle but customers are automatically programmed to say 'No,' or 'No thank you, I'm fine.' A 'no' answer to 'Do you have …?' gives you the opportunity to make another sale. 'No' to 'Do you need …?' or 'Do you want …?' firmly closes the door and you cannot pursue the matter further.

Too small

She's a size 28 and holding a skirt that says 'free size' on the label. You know this means roughly size 10 to 16. She asks to try it on. What do you do? It is never going to fit.

First and foremost, be tactful. If appropriate, you can say that skirt is too tight on you. 'It is amazing how the sizes all come up slightly differently.' Keep a tape measure handy and offer to find one in her size. If you know you have nothing suitable then offer to source what she is looking for or suggest an alternative shop.

The customer is always right

One day a customer came out of the changing room wearing a pair of skin-tight, Lycra leggings that flared out at the ankles, printed in a rainbow of psychedelic blobs. They were a slim-fit; she was not. They looked hideous; she was ecstatic. She bought them. What could I say?!

LABELLING THE GOODS

Equipment for labelling

Customers, especially ones who are new to your shop, are notoriously shy about speaking to shop assistants. In my experience customers do not buy unless they know how much something costs, so do not lose sales by failing to have prices clearly marked.

For clothing and other fabric items you will need:

◆ tagging gun with spare needles;
◆ kimble tags;
◆ kimble tags with hooks (optional);
◆ swing tag labels – No 9 perforated stock control tickets (see below);
◆ swing tag reduced labels.

No 9 perforated stock control tickets are small cards, approximately 40 x 60 mm, with a perforation across the middle and a hole punched in the top. They are attached to fabric and 'swing' by a short length of plastic (a Kimble tag), fired through the cloth by a tagging (or Kimble) gun. They can also be attached by a plastic loop, twisted round the item and fastened onto itself. Kimble tags can be bought with a hook on one end for hanging the tagged item. If using these, ensure that they are attached in such a way that they will not damage the goods.

The cards have four printed lines on each half of the ticket to enable you to record details of:

◆ code number
◆ style
◆ size
◆ price.

I use the back of the card also to record colour, supplier and date purchased. The same information is entered on both halves of the card.

At the moment of sale, the bottom half of the card is torn off and put into the till. Having this information on the label helps you know exactly what has sold and you know:

◆ what to replace from your storeroom each day;
◆ which items are selling well and need to be ordered;
◆ at sale time, when you want to reduce heavily the items that were bought a long time ago, which ones to reduce and by how much.

In addition the processes of exchange, refund and then returning the item to stock, are speeded up should a customer return the item, as the top half of the card remains on the item.

These cards can also be used as stock cards for anything that is sold in its box, as the card can be put into the box for removal at the moment of sale.

For non-fabric items you will need:

◆ price gun
◆ price gun labels
◆ sticky dumbbell labels
◆ sale labels.

A single-line price gun is perfectly adequate, although some price guns can print up to three lines of code and prices. The guns can be fitted with a stamp to show the company name but this is not necessary. Some will number sequentially and are used for quality control, shade marking, batch or industrial component numbering.

Price gun labels are usually yellow or white and come plain or printed with 'price', 'sale' or 'reduced'. I use plain yellow as they stand out clearly. They come in varying degrees of stickiness and the choice depends on what you are selling. If the item is delicate, eg hand painted, you will want a peelable label. A permanent label will pull the paint off, if it comes off at all.

Sticky dumbbell labels are self-adhesive paper labels in the shape of a dumbbell. The price (or other information) is written on the ends and the label is folded in half to form a loop attached to the item. These are useful for pricing items that will not easily accept a price gun label. Jewellers use 'elephant hide' labels. These are the same type of dumbbell labels but made from a very strong material so that they cannot be torn off. They are grey in colour, hence the name. These are designed for attaching to rings but can be used anywhere a strong label is required.

Ideally, customers can see at a glance exactly how much an item costs, but for the sake of the piece itself it is usually safer to stick the price underneath or on the back.

Both sticky and swing tags will be needed for sale labels. They are used not only for a general sale throughout the shop but also for reducing individual items at any time. There are always items that are delivered to you broken (and cannot be sent back to the supplier for replacement or credit), or become damaged in the shop or stockroom. Almost without fail, I have found that if such items are reduced in price customers will snap them up. Everyone loves a bargain!

If the item being reduced is damaged or faulty, write the details on the sale label and confirm them with the customer at the time the purchase is being made. That way the customer cannot bring the item back demanding a refund because of that defect.

PRICING: HOW MUCH TO SELL THINGS FOR

The standard mark up for giftware and clothing is 100% of the wholesale price including VAT, or 2.35 times the wholesale price excluding VAT. This is then rounded up or down to the nearest pound (or 99 pence).

For example, an item bought wholesale for £1.25 plus VAT of £0.22 = £1.47. Double this and the retail selling price is £2.99. This is the same as multiplying £1.25 by 2.35.

Jewellers mark up at least three to five times what they buy for. Sunglasses used to be a phenomenal ten times mark up but swag shops now sell exactly the same items at a lower mark up, so this is no longer possible.

When marking up an item, consider the following:

◆ What are your costs, location and market?
◆ What price are your competitors selling at?
◆ Can you make most money by marking up to the highest price possible and generating the greatest profit?
◆ Will the item sell faster at a slightly lower price and thus make most money through higher volume?

◆ TIP ◆

The selling price needs to cover the cost of buying the item, the running costs of the business and make a profit for you to pay yourself.

Price breaks

Items marked down to a better price break point will usually sell faster, eg £14.99 as opposed to £15.99. I tried this with two virtually identical skirts. I bought them wholesale for £6.50 each and sold one for £14.99, the other for £16.99. The £14.99 skirt outsold the £16.99 skirt by ten to one.

Promotions

Think about having a promotion on certain items to increase sales in general.

◆ EXPERIENCE ◆

'99p each or three for £2' was an offer I ran on nail varnish one summer. I was buying at 30p and selling quite happily at 99p but nail varnish, and this brand in particular, was very trendy. The shop had not been open very long and to boost the shop's profile, I decided to use this as a promotion.

The first day sales went through the roof. It brought in many, many new customers, making the shop very well known in the area. Sales of all other goods also increased, as most people would come in to buy their three nail varnishes (or multiples thereof!) and buy other things whilst they were in the shop. It really got me up and running.

Something for nothing

Sunglasses provide such a good profit that it is worth throwing in a free case. The cheapest cases only cost about 10p. Customers think they are getting something for nothing, go away happy and will come back again.

Low prices versus sale prices

I have always operated in a price conscious area. I once overheard a woman outside the shop saying, 'Their clothes are so expensive in there.' As we sold leggings from £1.99, and skirts and blouses from £4.99, I wondered what she considered cheap?

Keeping prices as low as possible has always been very important and has gained my shops good reputations for giving value for money. For some items, however, I have found that sales increase most when prices are reduced for a specific Sale rather than initially selling at the same, lower price. Sale labels and signage catch people's attention. This makes customers think they are getting a bargain, which is good for business.

◆ EXAMPLE ◆

Ethnic summer clothes are good value but with the unpredictability of the British weather, it is highly likely that many of them will end up being sold at a reduced price. To allow for this, consider initially marking up by more than 100% (say £11.99 instead of £9.99) and putting a sale or special offer on selected lines throughout the summer (reduce to £9.99 or offer two for £20). This 'Sale' could result in a greater turnover with bargain hunters boosting turnover.

Whatever mark-up you work to, you must to adhere to the 28-day rule. This allows you, the trader, to claim a reduction on products which you may wish to include in a sale or other promotion, but requires that the product must have been sold at a higher price for a period of 28 consecutive days within the previous six months in that outlet.

DISPLAY

Descriptions
If what you are selling has a story to it, make labels for each item giving details as well as the price. This really does improve sales.

Dreamcatchers, for example, are circular webs with feathers dangling below. The information label explains that they are made by North American Indians to protect themselves from bad dreams. Legend says that if you hang a dreamcatcher above your bed your dreams will be caught in the web. The good ones come down the feathers to you, whilst the bad ones disappear with the morning sun.

Semi-precious stones can be packaged individually with details of the name of the stone, star sign and birth month represented (these are not always the same) and information about what the stone can be used for. For example, 'Amethyst is said to aid sleep and relieve pain. It is the zodiac stone for Pisces and February's birthstone.'

People like to know exactly where things come from so the ethnic origin should be included when known. For example, soapstone carvings from Kenya, wooden masks from Zambia.

American tourists in particular often ask to buy something that has been made in Britain or comes specifically from your area.

Finding your hot spots

A hot spot is an area of the shop that naturally focuses the customer's attention and is particularly good for making sales. A classic example is the end of the aisle in a supermarket, which you face as you come in the door. This is where the supermarket manager will have the week's offers.

Where yours are will depend on the shape and layout of your shop. There are three basic shop layouts:

◆ **Grid:** where the aisles are parallel and perpendicular to each other, as used by supermarkets. This uses the space most efficiently but is not very exciting.
◆ **Freeform:** this is an informal layout, typically used by small or specialist shops. It can be flexible or may be dictated by the shape of a small shop or the type of goods being stocked.
◆ **Boutique:** where the shop is divided into separate areas each with its own scheme, to create unique shopping environments. Quite a large shop floor area is required to use this layout successfully but it is very good for creating hot spots and highlighting product lines.

It is commonly said that the area on the counter beside the till is a hot spot, but I have generally found that things do not sell well from here. Customers are not inclined to browse when they are under close supervision from the shop assistant. It can, however, be a good area for keeping low-priced, impulse buy items that need to be demonstrated. Remember woodpeckers on a stick? These have been around for many, many years but were made a must-have fad item when Chris Evans included them on his television show *TFI Friday*. Sales were made even better by keeping one on the counter for frequent demonstrations.

Making an impact

Display can help make an impact. Dressing a window with drapes of fabric or putting items on to rotating stands draws attention to a particular product or range of products. Buying bespoke display accessories can be expensive so learn to improvise with what you have to hand:

◆ Tins of tomatoes (with the labels removed), from the smallest up to catering-sized and bought in your local supermarket, make shelf supports in display cabinets.
◆ Paper clips can be twisted to create hooks to hang stock or labels from.
◆ Plant pots and wicker baskets from the local £1 shop make cheap and effective holders for small items of stock.

Sometimes the product itself will be used to create the impact, such as in a supermarket when one brand of baked beans is promoted by stacking the cans to build a giant pyramid. For this type of display to be successful you will need extra stock to sell, so make sure this product is going to be a really big seller or you will end up with a lifetime's supply in your stockroom.

A very good way to keep products prominent within the shop is to use display material that has been specially produced for that product by the manufacturer. This could be a cardboard cut out featuring an enlarged picture of the product or a plastic moulded display stand to feature every item in the range. Such point of sale publicity and display material is always worth having, particularly as they are often free. They have usually been researched and designed by marketing experts to make the best impact and the display stands will save you many headaches in trying to display the products to show them at their best.

◆ EXPERIENCE ◆

I bought a range of perfumes, initially concentrating on the six fragrances I knew would be the best sellers. Sales were disappointing, especially as I knew these scents were popular. Soon afterwards, the manufacturer brought out a floor-standing display, which held all ten of the fragrances produced in this range and incorporated a cupboard for holding spare stock. I bought the stand plus the four new fragrances and sales went shooting up. People had not known I stocked this brand of perfume when it was lost in the mêlée of the shop. The display stand did its job and brought the perfume to customers' attention.

With small stands for displaying ranges of figurines, I have even sold the stands to customers who want them to display their own collections at home.

Achieving the right lighting

Lighting is very important in a shop:

◆ Fluorescent strips give good background lighting but it is a very cold and harsh light.
◆ Spotlights focus attention on particular items or areas of the shop but on their own will leave pools of shadow in between.
◆ Low voltage halogens are a good source of light but must be used in large quantities or a further source is required to supplement them and increase the brightness.

> **◆ TIP ◆**
>
> Use a combination to make the shop as bright as possible. The more easily customers can see your displays, the more people you will attract into the shop.

If it is possible for you, sell lampshades! Hanging them from the ceiling brings that sales space into play. You can use low energy light bulbs, which will help to light your shop and be economical to run.

Positioning the products

If you stock a product that is slow or not selling at all, move it to a different location. It might be too low or too high. If people cannot see it – if it is not 'in their faces' – it can discourage sales. Equally, moving your best seller to a different part of the shop can kill sales totally.

Showing prices

The price marking order of 2004 requires that the selling price be clearly displayed on all products being sold by retailers to consumers. Retailers with an internal sales/display area not exceeding 280 square metres and itinerant traders (market stall-holders and barrow traders in shopping centres) are exempt from this requirement.

The price must be clearly legible, unambiguous, easily identifiable and inclusive of VAT and any additional taxes. Prices can be shown on the goods themselves, on a ticket or notice near to the goods, or grouped together with other prices on a list or catalogue in close proximity to the goods. Customers should not have to ask for assistance in order to be able to see a price.

Windows and similar displays, which contain items that can be removed and sold to customers, must display selling prices unless the items are purely promotional and not for sale. Special requirements apply where consumer and staff safety may be compromised by the display of particular high value products, ie items of jewellery, watches and precious metal with a selling price in excess of £3,000.

The law aside, it is to your own benefit to ensure all the products are clearly priced, including those in the window. Potential customers will generally walk out (or not come into the shop at all) rather than ask the price. Trading Standards officers will make regular, unannounced inspections of your shop and this is one of the things they check for.

Quantities

Unless it is being used to create a special display, only have as much stock out on display as will be sold in two days, but restock at the end of every day.

There is no point in having 50 of something on display if you only sell two a month. The excess will become damaged and dirty, taking up space that could be occupied by something more profitable.

SHELVING AND CABINETS

Slat Wall

As discussed in Chapter One, this is by far my favoured display system for flexibility but was too expensive an investment when I started up. Initially I used cheap pine shelving units from B&Q. To adjust the height of a shelf I had to take all the stock off, unscrew the unit from the wall, take the whole thing apart and put it all back together again. Holes had to be drilled and rawl-plugged in the walls for displays to be hung and every change was a major disruption as inevitably new lines of stock did not fit into the existing shop layout. Eventually, piecemeal, I fitted both the shops with Slat Wall. It has been more than worth it as Slat Wall enables a quick, relatively pain-free change around.

Glass cabinets

There are many companies manufacturing and supplying expensive retail cabinets. Ikea have a large range of cabinets and shelving at a fraction of the cost, together with low voltage halogen lights, which can easily be fitted to light the shelves. These are ideal for a small business setting up and widely used by wholesalers. A visit to a trade show can feel like a walk round one of Ikea's showrooms.

Shelves

Widest at the bottom and narrowest at the top of the wall will enable customers to see what is on all the shelves. Ensure stock is always pulled to the front of the shelf until you are able to restock. Labels should be turned to face forwards.

Suppliers' display stands

These will become dirty and tatty after a couple of years' use. This particularly applies to the spinners of postcards, greetings cards or window prints that usefully stand outside shops every day, to draw customers in. Some sales reps will regularly change the entire stand of stock – keeping best sellers but including new designs – and send a new, free display to freshen up sales.

The wind can be a problem for such outside displays. When the products hang from prongs, they can be blown off the stand unless secured from one prong to the next by elastic bands. Ensure also that the casters are removed from stands that are used outside – many a windy day has seen me having to chase my spinners down the High Street until I learned how to stop them blowing away.

USING THE SPACE

Look at your competition in the High Street. Shops such as The Gadget Shop, Dorothy Perkins or Burtons have all of their stock within a band around the centre of the walls, a couple of feet off the floor and up to head height. This is the ideal selling space and things will sell from this band much better than anywhere else in the shop. A small retailer, however, pays high rent per square foot for a half decent location, and to make the shop work must use every square inch of space.

The big chains will be getting much better price breaks than you, so maximise your business by using everything: the floor, up the walls, across the ceiling, down the windows. If you can hang something from it or rest something against it, use that space.

The audible space in the shop is also a sales opportunity. Licences are required to play music – the radio or even your own CDs – if it is there to provide background music, but some music labels do not need a licence and you can play what you are selling (see 'Useful Contacts' page 200). This promotes sales, which generates more income, whilst enhancing the atmosphere of the shop.

Vary the layout of the shop
Change your shop around regularly.

- Monthly, change specific display areas of the shop.
- Annually have a complete change (there will be some areas which are fixed but move everything else).

People see things afresh when in a different location and will often say, 'Oh, this is new. I didn't know you stocked that!' when sometimes it is something you have had for years and are trying to get rid of.

Window displays
Shops like Boots the Chemist and New Look do not put any window display in at all. They use posters showing price discounts or pictures of the latest product, often to tie in with a television or newspaper advertising campaign.

Hamleys, the London toyshop, is renowned for putting on elaborate displays with Disney or nursery rhyme characters which move to attract shoppers and their children every Christmas.

Somewhere between these two extremes is where you should aim. To put nothing in the window is a cop out and it is a waste for small businesses to do this.

◆ TIP ◆

Your window is your opportunity to show the outside world what you sell.

If you are not artistic then do you know someone who is? An artistic friend coming in one evening every two to four weeks would be of great benefit to the business. Alternatively, a professional window dresser may be available to do occasional work for you.

Whatever you do, make sure that:

◆ your display is clean and there are no cobwebs, dust or dead flies;
◆ the window is tidy and goods face outwards so passers-by see an attractive presentation;
◆ everything is clearly priced;
◆ it is well lit;
◆ the arrangement is changed regularly.

If your window is in the sun, ensure all products that are susceptible to fading are changed before the light affects them.

Updating the shop

Take photographs of the shop every six to twelve months. Refer back to them occasionally to see what was being stocked, how things were laid out and consider whether takings have gone up or down since.

ADVERTISING

Unless you can quantify and prove the benefit, conventional advertising is generally not worth the cost for small retail businesses. However, there are other ways to promote your shop.

A-boards outside the shop

These are the advertising display signs that can be seen from down the street to attract people in. They are easy to make: two rectangles of plywood, hinged at the top, with a cross piece halfway down the side to lock them and stop the boards sliding flat onto the ground. This cross bar forms them into an 'A' shape from the side, hence the name. Use them to advertise specific lines or offers. Paint them to match your shop colours and with the modern vinyl-cut sign writing, the information on the boards can be changed regularly at a reasonable cost.

Handbills

Print A5 flyers. These can be used to advertise:

◆ a new shop opening;
◆ specific lines;
◆ special events;
◆ other promotions.

Including an offer, such as '5% discount with this coupon', enables you to measure the success of the promotion.

◆ TIP ◆

Handing out the flyers in town, or putting them on car windscreens in local car parks, can attract new customers. One in every carrier and paper bag offers a reward to existing customers.

Local newspaper

Your local reporter is always looking for topical events to cover, such as the opening of a new shop in town. Develop contact with this person and keep them informed about your public relations activities.

Point of sale

Visual point of sale refers to merchandising equipment such as posters and other advertising signs, leaflet dispensers, general display accessories such as cubes, blocks or plinths for standing an item on, or specific display stands for the likes of jewellery, mobile phones or magazines. This is important, as good visual displays can increase sales. Signs that inform customers about the product or draw it to their attention will also increase sales of that product. Professionally produced signs will have the greatest effect on sales, but handmade signs are still effective in persuading customers to buy.

Electronic point of sale refers to computer hardware such as barcode printers and readers, credit card readers and receipt printers that, together with computer software, are used to track details of products stocked and sold. This equipment may be desirable but is not necessary to the running of a successful small business. It is an expense that can be delayed until the business is up and running.

Printed carrier bags

This is excellent advertising. Everyone who spends any money in your shop then walks round town advertising for you. Printing is a small cost, as you will need to have carrier bags anyway.

For a small shop starting up, the best carrier bags are ones that are simple, with clear printing to show the name and address of the shop. Go for the cheapest plastic bags that will be strong enough to carry the heaviest items you sell.

Try to keep to one size of bags. If you have a range of very large items, it may be more cost effective to stock a larger size of bag but not have it printed. I use black bin liners for the occasional extra-large, oddly sized item. This does not offend customers.

Small items are best put in paper bags as customers will generally put them in their pockets or other bags, and your money spent on printed bags will be wasted.

Choose a visible colour that is easy to read and which stands out. Mine are yellow, printed with black. This fits with the shop colour schemes but is also the most easily-read colour combination, as used by the AA.

Another reason for printed carriers is that it really gives you a kick when you walk down the street and see every other person carrying your bags!

Sponsorship/community public relations activities

Many of my products are aimed at the trendy, alternative market and I have contributed annually to the sponsorship of a local music festival. This is less for the coverage the subsequent advertising gives me, and more to help ensure such activities continue in the town. Events of this kind bring in both locals and outside visitors, many of whom will look round the shops whilst they are in town and return on subsequent shopping trips.

You will be asked to support every charity event that goes on in the area, from children asking you to sign their sponsorship forms, to organisers of fairs and fêtes and even the local council requesting corporate sponsorship. You will be asked for donations of time, money and raffle prizes. It is impossible to support every cause – believe me, you will be approached up to half a dozen times a day just by people coming into the shop on the off chance – but I believe it is important to support the local community as well as a number of charities that are close to my heart. And donating prizes for charity raffles or taking part in a charity fashion show need not cost you a great deal of money but will get positive publicity for your business.

Sticky address labels (able labels)

Have these printed with the shop address and stick on the bottom/back of everything you sell. That way, everyone will know where the item came from and where to buy more, even if it has been given as a present or won as a prize in a raffle.

Students

If there is a local college, consider offering a discount to students on production of their student union card. Advertise this offer in their college magazine or on the college notice board. If you stock the right products, at the right price, however, these people will come and buy from you anyway.

Wear it and use it

If you sell clothes, wear them yourself and give staff discount to encourage your employees to do the same. Consider providing outfits for staff to wear at work. I have sold many items when passers-by have seen what I am wearing, come in and bought it. The same applies to cosmetics and jewellery.

Yellow Pages telephone directory

If you are a retail shop selling giftware there is no need to spend money on one of their adverts (I have had this confirmed by one of their best salesmen). Telephone directory advertisements are excellent if you are a plumber, decorator or other tradesperson but not for a retail shop. Your advertising budget is spent on the location of your shop and the display in your shop window.

Anyway, most calls to the shop are people trying to sell *you* something – usually health insurance, life assurance or new cars. Offering to reduce the cost of your business rates (for a fee) was very popular a couple of years ago. I think the only sales call I have not had in the shop are for double-glazing.

ATTRACTING CUSTOMERS

Make as much use of the senses as possible to encourage people to come in and buy from you.

Sight

Have displays in the windows and inside the shop which attract the eye and draw people in to look around.

Sound

Play music in the shop which can be heard out on the street, drawing people in and then encouraging them to linger once they are in the shop.

Smell

Food shops obviously have the advantage, with bread-making machines for producing hot baguettes, ovens for cooking jacket potatoes, or coffee machines, all of which produce lovely aromas. These can be directed out into the street to tantalise people's sense of smell. Scented candles, pot pourri, or beauty products can all be placed near the door so that people can smell them as they approach the shop. An assistant walking around the shop (or even outside if this appropriate) offering free tests of a new perfume will advertise that product and increase sales.

Touch

Much as it is very annoying to have children wiping their sticky hands over everything, your turnover will slump dramatically if you do not allow potential customers to touch, pick up, and handle as much of your stock as possible. The only exceptions to this are for very valuable, easily stolen items and those that are too fragile to cope with repeated, often clumsy, touching. Many products are very tactile and it is only by feeling them that their appeal is appreciated. Stress balls, 'slime' and the slinky are all regular top sellers that would sit on the stockroom shelves forever if they were boxed and customers could not touch them.

Taste

By and large this is not appropriate, unless of course you sell food products.

INCREASING SALES

There are basically just two ways to increase sales.

1. Increase the number of potential customers coming through your door.
2. Do more with the people who are already coming into your shop.

The first option involves relocating, opening more shops, renovating your existing premises, advertising or increasing stock levels. These are all expensive and there is no guarantee that any of these measures will be particularly effective.

The second option again offers two choices. Either increase the closing ratio (sell to more of the people who are already coming into your shop) or increase the average sale (get each customer to buy more goods and spend more money). Either way, this is about improving the service that you give. By using the methods discussed in this chapter you should be able to maximise your sales potential without incurring the costs of expansion.

4

UP AND RUNNING

There are various mantras which I believe must be followed to make the business work to its full potential. I have tried to leave the soapbox in the cupboard whilst writing them but you must excuse me where it has crept out and crawled under my feet. I will start where I feel most strongly.

BE OPEN!

This is the most important factor in having a good day's trading. Unless you are open there is no business. I cannot emphasise this enough.

♦ TIP ♦

Have a sign on the door to inform customers what your opening hours are. These should be in line with standard trading hours.

My opening hours are: 9.30–5.30 Monday to Friday, 9–5.30 Saturday,
10.30–4.30 Sunday.

Opening time

When I first started trading, I opened at 9 am. As a holiday resort, the
town is not an early riser and as a sole trader needing to get to the bank
several times a week, I soon changed this to 9.30 am. Saturday is the
exception because it is busier, and the bank is closed anyway. 9.30 am is
later than the High Street shops' hours but it is acceptable given the location – most of the neighbouring shops also open at 9.30 am.

The important thing is I am always ready and open at 9.30 am sharp (earlier if I am in the shop and not working in the stockroom).

Customers at that time of day have often made a special trip to make a
specific purchase, possibly on their way to work. They cannot afford to
hang around. I have picked up many sales (some of them very generous
ones) when another shopkeeper has not bothered to get out of bed on a
winter's morning and their customer has waited outside in the cold hoping
someone will turn up. Eventually the customer has come into my shop to
keep warm, to ask if I know what time the other shop will open and generally have a moan. As they stand there, they look around at what I sell and
eventually, when they can waste no more time, they buy a different present
to the one they had planned. They will come back to me next time they
need something because they got a warm welcome; they will possibly not
go back to my rival.

Closing time

I started by closing at 6 pm but this is later than the High Street shops, and
the town is very quiet by then, particularly in winter. In summer, however,
tourists especially are in no hurry to go home so I keep the shop open for
as long as there are people looking round.

Sunday

The Sunday Trading Act of 1994 limits shop opening hours for shops over 280 square metres (or 3,000 square feet). There are no restrictions for shops below this size. The act does not regulate the sale of particular goods, but the sale of certain goods, such as alcohol, are subject to separate legislation.

I do not open on Sundays from after Christmas through to Easter but, especially being a seaside resort, have always found it worthwhile being open the rest of the year.

The harder you work, the more you will earn from the business, and the more hours you are open, the better your profits will be. The shop rent is the same whether you open six or seven days a week, so all you really have to cover on Sundays is the cost of wages.

Lunch time

This is the busiest time of a weekday. Between 11.30 am and 2 pm workers take their lunch breaks and will nip to the shops to make essential purchases or browse round to fill the time. This is not the time for you to close and slope off to eat your sandwiches.

> **◆ TIP ◆**
>
> If you do not have staff, then bring your food in with you and eat it at a quiet time. If you must close the shop, go before 11.30 am or wait till after 2 pm.

My local hardware shop closes for an hour and a half at lunchtime every day. The numerous staff all troop out together and come back together. I know, because 1.02 pm is the time I invariably drive up, desperate to buy an item of hardware that I have just run out of and cannot finish my current project without! In the 21st century you would have thought one of them could have thought to stagger lunch breaks. They also close for a half-day on Wednesdays – again my favourite time for needing to make a purchase.

RESPOND TO CUSTOMERS' NEEDS

Whoever is working in a shop, whether it is the proprietor, manager or the most junior member of staff, is a shop assistant – there to assist. One customer's money is worth the same as that of any other customer. Every chance you have to talk to someone gives you the opportunity to develop a relationship and increases your potential to make sales.

◆ EXPERIENCE ◆

Many items are extremely tactile and scented candles were all the rage at the time; some fragrances were clean and sharp, others sweet and mouth-wateringly tempting. Apple, honeysuckle, jasmine, lemon, pinecone, strawberry and vanilla, there were new flavours every few weeks. One man who was blind used to come in every week to 'see' and smell what was new. Leading him round, and helping him find out what things were, made me look at each object in a different light. I was able to stop and take time to appreciate each individual fragrance. He was a very good customer but that was secondary to the enjoyment his visits gave me – I hope the feeling was reciprocated.

Some customers have greater needs than others and it is your job as a shop assistant to anticipate those needs and respond accordingly.

Fractious children

I often have parents come into the shop to consider making specific purchases (as opposed to just browsing around) but sometimes their young children are so restless and complaining that they are unable to concentrate.

◆ TIP ◆

Instead of delivering your best sales pitch to the adults, it makes more sense to distract the youngsters and give their parents some peace to think.

I have wind-chimes and mobiles hanging from the ceiling and these can be set in motion to get very young children's attention; slightly older ones like to look for their own name on the spinners of personalised key-rings and pens that I stock. If your particular stock does not lend itself to this, then keep some toys under the counter for these situations – it can save a lot of breakages to your stock as well as helping to close the sale.

Be one step ahead and make an early move

It is not just the old or infirm who have difficulty in reaching for what they want; people carrying heavy bags, grasping onto their children, or the seemingly young and healthy, suffering from unseen sports injuries, all appreciate a helping hand. If someone is looking at an item that they cannot reach on their own, do not wait to be asked; fetch your steps and hand it down from the top shelf for them to look at properly; open the cabinet and hand it out to them; lift it up off the floor or clear space around it for them to view it more easily.

If someone is in a wheelchair or pushing a double buggy round the shop, save them any embarrassment of getting caught on something and quietly move any items that could be in the way.

Do not discriminate

The law states that guide dogs may bring their owners into any shop but in this country other dogs are not allowed into areas where there is food. As I do not sell food I encourage all dogs to bring their owners into the shops. The owners appreciate this and regularly spend money. There have never been any problems, such as little accidents on the carpet, and the bottle of disinfectant that I keep under the counter has only ever been used to clear up after children.

Know your suppliers

When a customer says, 'It's very nice but I was looking for a bigger one,' you need to be able to say, 'I know where to get one for you. I will find out the price and call you today. So long as the supplier has it in stock, I can have it in the shop for you by the end of the week.'

DISABILITIES DISCRIMINATION ACT

If you provide a service to the public, you have obligations under the Disability Discrimination Act. You cannot refuse to serve a person with a disability or provide a lower standard of service to someone because of their disability. You also need to make reasonable changes to the way in which you provide your services to ensure that you do not discriminate against such customers. This includes making reasonable adjustments to any physical barriers that may prevent people using your service or providing your service by a reasonable alternative means, such as bringing your goods to the person or helping them find items. These are some examples of the type of adjustments you could make:

♦ Ensure your premises are well lit and provide clearer signs.
♦ Provide an induction loop for a person with a hearing impairment.
♦ Provide seating.
♦ Install a permanent ramp and a handrail at the entrance to a building where there are steps.
♦ Replace a door handle with one that is easier to reach and to grip.
♦ Meet a mobility-impaired person in a more accessible venue or even at their home if your premises can only be reached by a flight of stairs.

Before you start to panic about your old-fashioned and totally inadequate premises, the Disability Discrimination Act takes a common-sense approach for small businesses and only requires that you make changes that are 'reasonable'. There is no rulebook and it is appreciated that some organisations can afford to do more than others. It would not be expected, for example, that a small firm with a tight budget could undertake the same level of structural alteration that a big national company could easily finance. It is about what is practical in your individual situation, what resources you have and your attitude. You will not be required to make changes that are impractical or beyond your means but you and your staff must do what you can to help in each individual circumstance.

My shops are one small step up from the street level outside which can be difficult for wheelchair users. A ramp could cause other people to trip and I have not yet managed to persuade the landlord to make the major structural changes required, so I deal with it as follows:

- Users of lightweight, sporty wheelchairs can generally get into the shop unaided.
- The person's companion or a member of staff can bump the traditional type of wheelchair up and then back down the step.
- For heavy electric chairs, we take the shop outside.

There is many a time I have stood in the middle of the arcade holding a mirror for someone to see how a necklace looks when it is on, or clutching armfuls of trousers for people to choose the right colours. On one occasion I trotted in and out with a succession of wind chimes for a lady to choose from. I certainly made heads turn that day – it was quite breezy and both she and the rest of the town heard an excellent demonstration of all the different sounds they can make.

KNOW YOUR STOCK

What, where and how much

Know what you have in stock, where it is in the shop and what is in your stockroom. When a customer asks for something it is important not to dither around looking in ten different places. The same applies to the boxes they come in.

♦ EXAMPLE ♦

> When a customer asks if you have anything suitable for a ruby wedding present, you need to be able to show that customer everything that is red or relates to the number 40.

♦ TIP ♦

> You do not need to be able to remember every price. So long as you know where to find something, you can find the price – because obviously every item will be priced!

Keep records of what you buy

Set up a spreadsheet on the computer for each supplier you want to record. List all the items in the range down the side and the months of the year across the top. Each time you receive a delivery enter the figures onto the spreadsheet. When you do your stock checks you will see which items sell best and can order accordingly.

♦ EXPERIENCE ♦

When selling small items like jewellery, and there are so many pieces it is difficult and time consuming to do regular stock checks, I keep a record of what I have bought and score off each item as it is sold. When I come to place an order, I know what has sold quickly and should be re-ordered, as well as what has been in stock for a long time and will not be re-ordered.

The better your records are of what you buy, and therefore what you sell, the better you will sell that product. Knowledge creates sales.

Beware of having personal favourites

The more you know about what you have bought and sold, the more precise your future buying can be. Left to instinct, you will believe your own biases and buy more of certain colours or styles, believing these to be the best sellers. The reality may be very different and you will constantly be out of stock of, or not have in stock at all, the colours and styles that you do not favour.

Do not be afraid to try something different. Nowadays I choose the range that I believe will sell best and then throw in a couple of 'rogue' colours or styles just to see if they will sell. There have been several occasions when I have resisted buying what I think is grotesque or tasteless only to be proved wrong when I am finally persuaded to try some, or have been repeatedly asked for them by customers.

SUCCESS IS A QUESTION OF ATTITUDE

Focus on your objectives

If your attitude is just to have a 'nice little shop', the business is probably not going to be a major success. You achieve what you think about most in life and need to go into the venture with the assertive attitude of being a trader, a merchant, a retailer.

◆ **EXPERIENCE** ◆

A shop opened nearby selling high quality chocolates. Due to its location, the owner knew that the busy days would be at the weekend, and weekdays would be quiet. Instead of using the weekdays to work on ways to increase sales, such as: increasing the weekday trade to passers by, developing a mail order business, or supplying to trade customers such as hotels or restaurants, she decided to use this quiet time to study for a degree with the Open University. There was a regular trickle of people coming into the shop every day but they did not buy much. The upshot was that they disturbed her studies and the shop did not generate enough income to sustain the business and her personal living costs.

She ended up employing someone to work in the shop each day whilst she went back to her old job to earn enough to live off. As a result she achieved neither her goal of being self-employed nor of attaining her degree.

Competition

◆ **TIP** ◆

Competition is positive. It makes you work harder and stops you from becoming lazy.

It is disheartening if someone opens up next door to you selling the same type of products that you do – I know, because this has happened to me. The new person told everyone that he was going to put me out of business. A wise old sage advised me not to get sucked into that game and concentrate on my own business. I did that and took the following action:

◆ I spoke to my suppliers and where possible agreed sole rights of supply in the town. It is a small town and most suppliers were happy to ensure that one retailer did not sell their products at a discount to the detriment of another retailer.
◆ I was vigilant in sourcing goods at the lowest possible prices, the benefits of which I passed on to my customers.
◆ I sourced new lines, expanded the range of goods I stocked and looked for everything that was different, new and innovative.

Where I led, my competitor only followed. The end result was that the newcomer put himself out of business and my turnover went up. Other shops have opened up since, often selling similar lines to mine but never in out and out competition. We have always been careful not to compete with each other that directly – there is no need to after all, as there are plenty of different goods out there to be bought and sold.

ORGANISE YOUR TIME

However trite it may sound, time is precious and time is money. There is never enough of it in a day, so squeeze out the very last drops.

Make lists

Not just shopping lists for the supermarket, but daily to do lists, monthly lists of suppliers to ensure that each one is ordered from regularly and annual lists of what you want to achieve, both personally and professionally.

Do it now

Most small tasks are better done straight away whilst they are fresh in your mind. It takes twice as long to have to remember to do something or even to write it down to be done later. When the post comes in, deal with each letter as you open it. Do not put it in the in tray for attention later.

Doubling up/multi-tasking

Use every opportunity to do two things at once.

- When making a journey by public transport, read the latest trade magazines on the way.
- Write your planning list for the day when you are eating breakfast or better still, the night before whilst cooking supper. (I find that by writing down all the things I have to do it clears my mind, making it possible for me to get a good night's sleep.)
- Post your letters whilst taking the dogs for a walk or taking the children to school.

Delegate

This can be done sideways as well as downwards. If you are in partnership with someone but employ no staff, there are still opportunities for delegation: one person deals with the finances, the other with buying stock, one with display, the other with maintenance and repairs.

Avoid waste and temptation

- **Telephone calls**: keep conversations short and to the point. Use an egg timer on your desk to restrict you if you find this difficult.
- **Email**: these are even better for saving time than making telephone calls. There is no time wasted waiting for the phone to be answered, for the right person to come to the phone, or asking, 'How are you?' and other such pleasantries.
- **Meetings**: keep discussions focused and save trivial chatter for the pub after work.

Good is good enough

Set yourself a time limit to complete a task and do not keep re-working it. Once the bulk of the project is completed, the end result will probably not benefit from endless tweaking – you are really only procrastinating and avoiding what needs to be done next.

◆ **EXAMPLE** ◆

In writing this book, I could either keep tweaking it forever or decide it was good enough to submit to a publisher. It would either be accepted and the tweaking done afterwards or rejected and need a complete re-write.

GENERATE IDEAS

It is important to do this regularly and take the time to be creative.

- Sit quietly for 30 to 60 minutes. No coffee, no cigarettes, or music. After about 25 minutes your mind will clear and you will be able to come up with new ideas for whatever it is you are thinking about.

◆ Write your goal or aim at the top of a piece of paper in the form of a question. Then think of 20 ideas to solve this. The first five will be obvious, the second five will be hard and the last ten will be really difficult to think of but will be the most imaginative.

◆ EXAMPLE ◆

How can I increase sales by 20% over the next three months?

1. improve the window display
2. change the signage
3. run a promotion …

ADAPT TO CHANGE

Adaptability is key to success in life and in business.

From the 1960s onwards, small corner shops were taken over by Asian families who were prepared to open for business well into the evenings and at weekends. They saw a need from the changing lifestyles of British families, with people working full-time and unable to shop during office hours.

The supermarkets have followed their lead and now it is possible to shop 24 hours a day.

◆ EXPERIENCE ◆

My second shop was being run as a gift shop before I took it on. The owner spent six months watching my shop heaving with customers every Saturday whilst hers was steady on a good day. Business had been tailing off for her for the last few years and finally she decided to call it a day and closed her business after trading for close to 20 years.

One of the things she said to me as she cleared out and I prepared to move in was, 'people told me I should sell wind chimes but I thought I should stick to what I know'. Had she kept an open mind and evolved her business as the demands of the market wanted, she would not have watched her income slide and when the time came to retire, she could have sold the business for a profit instead of having to sell everything off for what she could get. A sad end to what my friends remember as *the* place to shop when they were children.

When change is foisted upon you do not waste time and emotional energy in concentrating on the problem. Instead focus on the solution and work out how you are going to make the best of it.

◆ EXAMPLE ◆

A proposed new road layout in the town diverting traffic away from you would have many shopkeepers raising protests to the council, writing letters and attending meetings, talking about nothing but the negative with family, friends and customers. In reality, there is little chance of changing such proposals so it is better to focus on the positives – the bus stops are to be moved closer to your shop, there will be better pedestrian access throughout the town with floral displays and more seating areas. Such changes will attract street entertainers, making the town a nicer place to be, and encourage more shoppers. Think of whom these changes are designed to appeal to and adapt your shop to cater for them. While the changes are settling in advertise your shop to people by handing out flyers in the town and to people getting off the buses.

◆ TIP ◆

If you start to address the solution as soon as you know that your circumstances or environment is to change, then you will have a head start on those who are still complaining by the time the change comes into force.

IF SOMETHING IS NOT WORKING, CHANGE IT

I have put together window displays that I think look great only to have fewer passers-by come into the shop, even though the rest of the town is busy. I have moved the shop around to create a more logical, accessible, attractive layout – and takings fall. In these circumstances do not hesitate – change things back to the way they were or to something entirely new.

There is a young student who walks past my shop every week. If the window display has changed she comes in. If not, she walks past.

◆ EXPERIENCE ◆

The town I trade in is fairly modern, brash and down to earth. It is not quaint or beautiful but has its own charm – more kiss me quick than architecturally picturesque.

After the 1990s recession there were empty shops and few shoppers. To boost trade the signposts, bench seats and rubbish bins in the town were painted bright blue and yellow. There was outcry. Newspaper articles were printed, petitions written and protests raised. The tasteful black and gold paintwork had to be restored.

Eventually mediocrity returned but not before people came flooding into town to see what the fuss was, boosting trade both then and since. A success for those with the blue and yellow paint cans, and for the saying that if something is not working, change it.

BE DIVERSE

Tempt people in

Having a wide selection of goods in your shop means that people have to come in to look around. Too often I see new ventures where people have such a limited selection of stock that it is possible to stand outside, eyeball the whole shop and walk away thinking, 'There is nothing in there for me'. You cannot accuse my shops of being like that! They are crammed full with a large variety of different products. The only way people can find out what I sell is to come in. Once they are in, I stand a very good chance of making a sale.

The fabric and flowers principle

'Fabric and Flowers' was the name of a shop, which sold just that. The flowers were pot pourri, dried flowers and also the prints on fabrics used to cover vases, bowls and other decorative objects. The owners also had a second shop where they designed and sold hand-tufted rugs.

The principle was that there were three prongs to this business: the flowers, the fabric and the rugs. One week, nobody would be interested in buying the dried flowers and pot pourri but it would not be a bad trading week because everyone wanted to buy the fabric covered bowls or the rugs.

Next week, it was the dried goods that everybody bought and the following week everything sold in equal quantities. This might sound far-fetched, but it really happens.

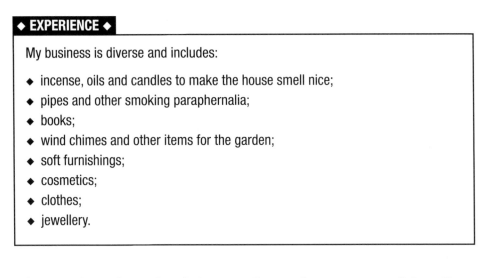

◆ EXPERIENCE ◆

My business is diverse and includes:

- ◆ incense, oils and candles to make the house smell nice;
- ◆ pipes and other smoking paraphernalia;
- ◆ books;
- ◆ wind chimes and other items for the garden;
- ◆ soft furnishings;
- ◆ cosmetics;
- ◆ clothes;
- ◆ jewellery.

There are busy days when I do not sell any of one or more of these lines, but I will still have a very good trading day.

DRAW ATTENTION TO YOURSELF

Anything that moves will draw the eye to it. Each summer I hang a giant twirling windsock in the shop doorway. It is multicoloured and hangs about three metres long from the top of the shop doorway. Everyone walks into it as they come into the shop and it is great for encouraging sales of the smaller, more manageable versions of the same item.

CREATE YOUR OWN MARKET

If you find a product that sells well, you can almost create your own market in it. People will come from all over the country to buy from you when they know you have the biggest range available and are the best supplier there is. This popularity will increase the interest of your other shoppers and sales increase.

MAINTAIN YOUR CORE BUSINESS

Best sellers are the lines that sell and sell and sell. Whatever else comes and goes fashion-wise, these are a must to keep in stock. They are your core business and help to form the identity of the business. This is what you expand from when times are good, and where you look back to if you need to re-establish your business when times are hard. Be faithful to them at all times and avoid taking the business off at a tangent.

Boots the Chemist was originally just that, a chemist. Nowadays Boots sells perfumes and cosmetics, electrical goods, develops your photographs and even provides your lunchtime sandwiches. The company has branched out with dental, optical and other health and wellbeing services. Some of their diversifications are now well established but others have been a struggle, and each time Boots has looked back to its core business of being a chemist.

◆ EXPERIENCE ◆

My core business and best sellers are:

- incense sticks, cones and the trays that hold them and catch the ash.
- smoking paraphernalia including rolling papers, pipes and 'baccy' tins.
- long billowing skirts with elasticated waistbands, and long fringed tops – many people who first wore them in the 1960s still wear them today and their popularity continues because they are excellent for accommodating all shapes and sizes!

CREATE THE RIGHT AMBIENCE

It takes a subtle blend of herbs and spices to achieve this. The objective is to make people want to stay in the shop rather than make their purchase and rush out straight away. If you do not have at least one person a day compliment you on the shop, you have got something wrong.

Fragrances

Even if you sell them, do not burn incense in your shop. This might seem like a good idea: lots of people like incense and it is a top selling line. Perhaps you think it smells good, and it advertises the fact that you sell incense.

But many people do not like incense and the smell will discourage people from entering your shop. Others will be unable to come in due to asthma or other breathing problems and you do not want to alienate any potential customers. Fragrance oils, aromatherapy oils and scented candles do not cause the same problem but the aroma from a shop that is well stocked with unlit and boxed fragranced products is quite strong enough for people to smell as they walk past the shop and will draw them in without the need for acrid smoke.

I never burn joss sticks but another shop in the town did. Customers used to come to me complaining that they would not go into the other shop because of the smell. The other shop went out of business!

Strawberry oil is the exception to this rule.

Anita Roddick used to use drops of strawberry oil to encourage people into her shop when she opened the first Body Shop. Studies have been carried out to show that the smell encourages customers to spend money. I used strawberry oil in an oil vaporiser behind the counter during my first year of trading and it certainly did not harm trade. I only stopped burning it because the area behind the counter became too crowded with stock and other paraphernalia to safely have a candle and hot oil burning all day.

Music

This is very important in creating the right atmosphere but it also affects physical behaviour. Music with a fast beat energises people, which is why it is played in health clubs and gyms. A faster beat encourages people to eat more quickly, so restaurants may find it helps to generate a fast turnover of tables.

Music with a tempo of 72 beats per minute or less is soothing and makes people slow down. It can encourage them to linger longer in shops. Classical music has been shown to be more effective than pop music in generating sales, with increases of up to 38%. New Age music is slow and relaxing. Much of it is based on classical music or on the sounds of nature.

Music can create a memorable identity but it is important to play the right sort. What is uplifting for one person is another person's dirge. You and your staff will have to listen to it all day, every day. The natural sound of bird song is very nice but running water will have you and your customers running to the toilet!

What to say

A customer asks, 'How's business?' One shopkeeper replies, 'Oh, could be better'. The other says, 'Yes, it's going great'.

Make sure you are the second shopkeeper.

> **♦ TIP ♦**
>
> Always talk in positive terms even if it has been pouring with rain all week and you have not seen a shopper for days.

The customer will think you must be doing something right and want to be associated with that success. They want to be able to tell their friends that they shop at the thriving store not the one that is going to the wall.

HAVE A HANDS-ON APPROACH

Encourage customers to touch the goods that they are interested in buying, including anything that you take out of a locked cabinet to show someone. Many items are very tactile and touching them brings another dimension to their existence – think about the soft caress of a velvet scarf around your neck as opposed to one made of wool that scratches and itches.

Touch enhances the sense of ownership. Think about a piece of jewellery – you try on a ring and can feel how smoothly the ring slides on and fits snugly between your fingers; the stone glistening and catching the light as you move your hand. There is a sense of loss as you take it off to hand back to the assistant.

KEEP STAFF BUSY

Some weeks of the year everyone is rushed off their feet and there is no time to think, let alone get all the daily jobs done. At other times of the year people are twiddling their thumbs, wondering what to do with themselves and saying, 'I'm bored'.

A typical day in a shop sees quiet periods in the early morning and late afternoon. This is the time when staff must get on with the unpopular but necessary jobs of cleaning because you need an empty shop whilst you strip down displays and dust them. Being busy is self-perpetuating, however, and if a shop is busy more people come in. The more people that come in, the more sales are made.

- If you look in a shop and see the assistant slouched over the counter looking uninterested, reading a book or filing her nails, does this encourage you to go in?
- When you see assistants busily working away, checking off invoices, unpacking products, arranging them on the shelves and writing out signs or labels, will this activity awaken your curiosity to go in and see what is new?

I also suggest that you would find the second scenario less threatening. Shop assistants who are occupied are not waiting to pounce on the first customer who walks through the door.

◆ EXPERIENCE ◆

I sell clear, hanging crystals in different shapes and sizes – the kind that are used for chandeliers. They are hung in windows to catch the sunlight and send rainbows spinning round the room. The supplier can provide these ready packaged but I buy them loose. When the shop is quiet, we attach clips and string up the crystals using silver thread. This makes them cheaper for me to buy so the profit margin is greater, and it keeps staff busy.

> **♦ TIP ♦**
>
> Never make assumptions about anyone's ability to understand what they see or are told. No matter what you say, someone will always interpret it in a different way.

Making it clear to customers

The music shop across the way from my shop moved next door to me. This was in a pedestrian walkway, so there was no busy street of cars between the old location and the new one. Before they left, the proprietors stuck posters in the window saying that they were moving and telling people where the new shop was.

I was stunned by the number of people who would walk up to the old shop, some even trying to push the door open, and stare bewildered before walking away. Others would turn around and come into my shop to ask if I knew what had happened to the music shop. Short of employing someone to stand in the street and direct customers to the new shop I do not think there was any way they could have got this right – we all just do not see things sometimes.

Giving clear instructions to staff

> **♦ EXPERIENCE ♦**
>
> A delivery of trinket boxes had come in. There was only one design, but they came in three different colours. I asked the Saturday girl to put a row of each colour on the shelf on the far wall. As I tidied the shelves later that afternoon I looked at what she had done. There was a row of blue boxes along the front of the shelf, a row of pink boxes behind the blue boxes, and a row of yellow boxes behind the pink boxes. What I had wanted was to see one blue, one pink and one yellow boxes at the front edge of the shelf, with each box having a line of boxes in the same colour behind.

BE AWARE OF TRENDS

There have been times when I have bought what is selling really well at the wholesalers in London and in friends' shops in other parts of the country.

But in my shop sales are as flat as a pancake. The question is, is it up to the minute or too far advanced? The provinces tend to lag behind London trends and I have often had to wait another season before certain lines sell at their full potential. Studded belts, wrist and collar bands (a revival of the punk era) were an example of this.

♦ TIP ♦

Check out your local high street. Make sure that what you want to sell is not already being well covered by the 'big boys'.

♦ EXPERIENCE ♦

Hair accessories were a big seller in my shop before a well-known accessories shop opened a branch in the town. I went into this line at the start of a big fad and pulled out as the fad was ending, which was shortly after this new shop opened. I made money on a low priced but (at the time) very fast selling item and then moved on to the next fad. I could not compete with the new shop, because there was only room in my shop for a fraction of the range that this specialist could stock, as it was only one line amongst many for me. Hair accessories is what my new competitor does. Although we bought from the same suppliers, this new shop was part of a big organisation, which would have been getting better price breaks than I could. (Incidentally, I was selling at lower prices than any other of my competition!)

I phased out this line because there was more profit for me to move on and devote the space to the next fad – which was belts.

KEEPING STOCK

If it doesn't sell

After the first few years of trading there will undoubtedly still be stock in the shop, or at the back of the stockroom, from the day you opened.

Cut the prices and get rid of it. If it has not sold in the last year it is unlikely to start selling now. It will only become grubbier and more damaged. Slash the prices if necessary and make space for something new that people will want to buy.

Storage is expensive

£15 per week will be your minimum cost for a lock-up garage that may not even keep out the damp or be secure from vandalism. Do you really need storage or are you just overbuying? If there are areas of your stockroom that have not seen the light of day for many years, you are buying too much and not clearing out old stock.

When importing, you will need storage. Initially costs can be kept down by using your loft, garage or garden shed at home, where you know the goods will be secure. When you need to rent additional space try to ensure the agreement is by a licence, not a lease. This maintains flexibility as your needs can change from one year to the next.

◆ EXPERIENCE ◆

I needed to rent an old barn as storage whilst I was importing large pieces of furniture. A change of circumstances meant I was able to store all my excess stock at home and the licence enabled me to terminate the agreement quickly.

There are many quirky old buildings once used by big manufacturing companies that have ceased to trade. Often the building is too old-fashioned to be used by one company again. The many rooms may be leased individually to small businesses, particularly those starting up. When the rooms are let on licence (not lease) the businesses can move to larger areas as they grow – and if times become hard or people have overstretched themselves, they can move back to a smaller space.

◆ TIP ◆

Sharing storage space can give great flexibility. Do you know anyone who is reliable and trustworthy, with a workshop that they may be able to let you use part of? This can be particularly useful during busy times of the year.

BE CLEAR ABOUT YOUR RETURNS POLICY

There are various ways of dealing with goods that customers return to a shop.

Faulty items

If the item is faulty, the customer has proof that it was bought from you, and it was purchased within a reasonable time scale then you can first offer to replace or repair it. If this is not acceptable then you must give a full refund.

◆ EXPERIENCE ◆

A customer returned a set of tarot cards in which there were two cards the same and one card missing. She wanted the cards replaced and as this was clearly a mistake by the manufacturer I changed them immediately. She checked the new pack before she left the shop. I returned the faulty cards to the supplier for another set.

◆ EXPERIENCE ◆

A woman returned a dress for a refund because it was faulty. I offered commiserations and apologised immediately but was suspicious that she did not want a replacement when the receipt showed she had only just bought it. The dress was the type that has a belt stitched into each side seam. She claimed the seam was coming apart but it was clear the belt had caught on the back of a chair or been yanked by a child; not only was the seam torn open but the fabric had been ripped. She admitted she had not bought it in that condition but was adamant it was faulty. I would not give a refund and directed her to Trading Standards; I heard nothing more.

Change of mind

Where a customer has changed their mind about the purchase and the item is not faulty, there is no entitlement to a refund. Any refund of money is entirely at the shop's discretion.

Some shops offer a no-quibble, full refund if the goods are returned within so many days. This can be a good way to make a sale, particularly for something like a digital camera, as customers know they can change their mind and so they do not feel pressured into buying. The shop knows that, in most cases, once the customer has taken it home and used it, he or she will be totally sold on its features and will not bring it back.

There is, however, no entitlement to a refund if the customer has damaged the article because of any misuse.

If you are going to accept returns, make sure that people know what your policy is. You may want to insist that:

♦ goods must be unused;
♦ in their original packaging;
♦ accompanied by proof of purchase.

When something is brought back, check that it is un-damaged. This is particularly important with clothes, when I have often had people buy a dress on Saturday, wear it that night and bring it back for a full refund on the Monday morning. The stench of cigarette smoke and perfume is a dead giveaway!

Any return must be accompanied by proof of purchase. Clothes from most of the big stores have their own labels in but what I sell is not necessarily exclusive to my shop. Proof of purchase can be the till receipt, credit card receipt or statement. I also like to see the goods returned in one of my bags.

♦ EXPERIENCE ♦

A teenager with no receipt came asking for a refund. His sister had stolen from their mum and they needed the money back before it was missed. I knew the item was not from my shop; it was a design I had never stocked. I explained this but he pleaded and argued, demanding his 'rights' and begging for mercy for his sister, who would be in 'big trouble'. Eventually he admitted that it came from my 'other branch'. I smiled and told him he should have mentioned that earlier. The relief on his face was enormous. Then I told him I didn't have another branch. He left without another word.

LEARN TO SAY NO

Every day, people come into the shop asking you to display their posters for forthcoming events, products that they sell and services that they provide. If you are a music shop this can be acceptable. Advertising gigs for local bands and the publicity material for album covers is in keeping with your shop, and may help to sell your products.

For other shops it is not a good idea. It looks messy and window space is needed to display the shop's own products and promotions. You pay a lot of money for rent and your window is your advertising space. A good window display will bring customers into the shop and it is *your* customers who pay *your* wages.

BUDGET FOR THE YEAR

Employees receive regular payments of the same amounts of money into their bank accounts each week or month. A shop's takings will never be that consistent.

Many gift shops claim that one third of their annual turnover comes from the Christmas trade, and most retailers find the first three months of the year are quiet, with takings considerably less than the rest of the year. This is traditionally the time to have a sale and clear out old stock. Inevitably this means that although turnover may seem good, profits will be down. It is important to allow for these factors in your business and personal budgeting.

KEEP HEALTHY

When I first opened in business I was in the shop every day until I found someone I could trust to be a key holder. I was open for trade six days a week, at the wholesalers on Sundays and fitting in the accounts and other paperwork in the evenings and early mornings.

◆ TIP ◆

As a sole trader, your income is totally reliant upon your own efforts, so it is very important to take care of your health.

Once you become self-employed it is amazing how many coughs and colds you do not fall prey to. On the odd occasions when you are ill, it will be in your own time and only after you have finished doing what you have to do. This might sound bizarre, but over the last few years I have only been ill after Christmas when business has quietened down, not in run up to the big day, or on the few Sundays when the shops are closed (in the first three months of the year). Somehow the body manages to keep going.

◆ EXPERIENCE ◆

One time I was ill whilst on a buying trip in the Far East and I was so unwell I had to ask the hotel staff to call out a doctor. Within half an hour he was there, accompanied by his nurse and three medical bags of tricks. After an extensive examination the diagnosis was given, the prescription written out and dispensed, together with clear instructions as to how and when to take what. 24 hours later they were back to check my progress, but I was gone. The medication had done the trick and I was well enough to be back at work.

I have not known the NHS to provide quite the same service so keep healthy. Eat lots of fresh fruit and vegetables and avoid the temptation to live off takeaways. Get yourself out into the fresh air and take regular exercise. There is no better way to keep stress levels down.

FAILING TO THRIVE

When you have been up and running for a few years there will be times when you find the business seems to be taking a bit of a down turn or slackening off. That is the time to re-assess what you are doing, look at all the areas of the business and bring it back to its core values.

So long as you have a core section of stock that will give you a good steady turnover, your business should continue to provide you with a good living.

Do not become self-indulgent

Don't tailor everything to your own personal taste. There was a strong fashion in the homeware market during the 1980s for chintzy Laura Ashley but in the 2000s it has been much more minimalist Ikea. Your business needs to take into account these trends even if they do not match with your own preferences. Remember you are buying for the general public, not your own home or wardrobe.

Do not over stretch yourself financially

If you have one particularly good trading quarter, it does not mean it's time to think about buying a new house at twice the mortgage.

Don't be greedy

Price your goods at a reasonable mark-up without being greedy. Customers will know if you are overpriced in comparison to your competitors and will go elsewhere.

Keep moving forward

Always be on the lookout for the next trend. To borrow a phrase from the theatre world: your business is only as successful as your last sale.

Stock that you have imported yourself should have cost you less than that which you could buy in the UK – where you are paying for someone else's profit. You should, therefore, be able to keep your prices low, to attract customers in and see off any competition.

Keep both the business and your domestic affairs tight financially and always ensure you have access to a good reserve of money should you need it.

Take care of the business and it will take care of you.

5

LOOKING AFTER THE MONEY

In this country it is very easy to set yourself up as self-employed. You should advise the taxman that is what you are going to do, but generally speaking there are no fees to pay, no taxes to be paid up front. Unless you are planning to sell something like alcohol, there are no applications to make and no licences required to trade.

A big problem for small businesses, and one that can lead to bankruptcy, is not allowing for taxes. When you are employed PAYE you do just that – you pay as you earn – but when you become self-employed it is easy to forget to put money aside for what has to be paid later.

Become organised and keep records. Ask for and keep receipts for every-thing you spend. File cash receipts in date order and invoices that have been paid by cheque by the number of the cheque; this makes for easy reference. Open a separate bank account so your personal dealings do not become mixed up with those for the business, and find yourself a good accountant.

ACCOUNTANTS

The services of a fully qualified chartered accountant will cost more than for one who is part qualified. Unless you are a limited company, you are unlikely to need to pay for the extra qualifications. The *Yellow Pages*, your local Business Forum or asking self-employed friends will soon lead you to the right person for you.

You choose how much work your accountant does for you, depending on your ability to keep records and your ability to pay their bill.

Year end books

I would recommend having an accountant to finalise and submit your annual self-assessment tax return. This should ensure that all means of tax avoidance are fully utilised, will give your books the credibility of the professional input and hopefully will ensure that any tax investigation is directed towards the poor innocent who has not used an accountant.

Other services

An accountant's services can include doing the wages or the VAT return, but it is all at a cost. These are routine tasks that you can easily learn. It would be much cheaper to try to do them yourself and pay the accountant to check your first attempts if you lack the confidence initially.

BANK CHARGES

Bank charges for small businesses are notoriously expensive. The Cruikshank Report (published in 2000) was commissioned by the government to investigate banking services for small businesses. It found profound problems in the industry, and to date little has changed. We all expect free personal banking nowadays but a small business can pay up to 70p for every transaction in or out of the account, with additional charges for every cheque or cash deposit made into your own account.

I was with one of the big High Street banks and paying approximately £50 per month in charges. A move to the Co-operative bank has reduced this to around £5 per month after receiving the interest they pay me on the account balance.

CHOOSING A BANK

There are a variety of bank accounts to choose from: High Street, telephone and Internet.

The High Street banks can rely on people banking with them out of habit and familiarity.

◆ They tend to be more expensive than other accounts.
◆ There will probably be a branch local to you, although the opening times will be restricted to weekday working hours and possibly Saturday mornings.
◆ Branches can be difficult to reach due to traffic congestion and parking restrictions.
◆ There should be cash point machines locally which increase access to your money.

Postal, telephone and Internet accounts cut their running costs by being out of town or abroad where staff costs are less.

◆ They pass these savings on to their customers so bank charges are lower.
◆ They have to compete harder to gain business, leading to more innovation with new products and services.
◆ You can operate the account from the comfort of your own home at whatever time of the day or night suits you. (For telephone accounts, however, do find one where the call is answered by a person rather than a machine because extended periods of time listening to their recorded music and choosing from endless lists of options will quickly drive you insane.)
◆ Cheques must be paid into the account by post (Royal Mail). I have never had any go astray but this is always a concern and I keep a log of every cheque sent, detailing the issuing bank and sort code, account holder and number, date written and the amount it is for.

- There is not always a way to pay cash into these accounts, so you may have to run a second account to pay cash into and then transfer it over. This will take longer for cash to reach the account than with a conventional bank account.
- Not all internet accounts issue cheque books, relying purely on electronic transfers in and out of the account.
- Internet accounts are great when both your computer and the bank's on-line facilities are working. If the site or your computer is down, you cannot view your account or transfer funds. This can happen at the most crucial of times and so is the deciding factor for me. I have a business postal account and make frequent use of Internet access to all my bank accounts but for a business account, which I need access to at all times, computers are just not yet reliable enough.

Overdrafts

Manufacturers and wholesalers generally have to offer customers at least 30 days credit, whereas shops receive payment at the time of sale. This facilitates a steady cash flow for shop owners, eliminating the need to run an expensive overdraft. All bank managers will encourage you to have an overdraft – it is easy money for them to earn – but for you it is just money down the drain. Control your costs and stay in credit from the day you start your business and you will save yourself a small fortune by the time you retire.

There are ways to minimise your bank costs.

- As a new business, look for an account that will give you at least one year's free banking, if not two.
- Before the end of the free banking period look at what other banks are offering to find the best possible service and value for money. Check moneyfactsonline.co.uk/mfBAF/root.sp to compare what is on offer.
- Make regular payments by standing order or direct debit. This is cheaper than writing a cheque.

It is good practice to keep up to date with what is available – from other suppliers, from your competition and especially from organisations that are providing you with a service that you pay for. Do not be complacent when it comes to banks – you would not pay ten times as much for your weekly groceries if the supermarket down the road sold everything that much cheaper.

BANK STATEMENTS

Ask for them weekly if you have approximately 25 or more transactions going through the account each week. 25 transactions is the maximum that will appear on one sheet of a normal bank statement. This makes it easier to keep track of the account and cuts down the risk of overdrawing the account by accident.

Reconcile the account each time you receive a bank statement to ensure that:

- the account does not go overdrawn;
- all transactions are correct;
- there are no 'extra' charges being made.

CASH

Take the week's takings with you to the wholesalers and save the cost of banking the money. Cash payments often attract a discount on the invoice.

If you do bank takings daily, then vary your route as much as possible, go at different times of the day and take turns with other members of staff to go to the bank. This reduces the chances of you being attacked on your way to the bank and the takings stolen. Although as they say on *Crimewatch*, 'don't have nightmares' about it. You are unlikely to be targeted and using basic common sense will reduce the possibility even further.

CHEQUES

Invoices come in throughout the month. Most will need to be paid in 30 days. File them in date order in a 'to pay' folder. At the beginning of each month sit down and write out the cheques for the whole month; this is more efficient than doing it each day. Put the cheques in their envelopes ready for posting. Date each envelope with the day it needs to be posted in order for the bill to be paid on time, and post accordingly. Use a bank reconciliation sheet to keep the bank balance up to date and ensure that the account does not become overdrawn.

CREDIT CARDS

Paying for stock by credit card

This can be quick and convenient. A personal card paid off in full every month will result in no extra costs. If it offers cash-back, you will earn money on your purchases. A business credit card on the other hand will incur an annual fee, a charge for every transaction and probably higher rates of interest.

Unless you are a limited company, you should be able to get away with using a personal card and as a small business I have never seen the personal benefit in having a business credit card. If you must have one, ensure that the bill is paid off in full each month, either by direct debit, incurring the lowest bank charge, or in cash at the bank for nothing.

Accepting payment by credit or debit cards

This is an absolute must. Few people use cheques nowadays and many do not carry much cash (if any). So, especially for those large impulse buys, arrange for a bank to provide you with merchant services. This can be arranged with any High Street bank, and does not have to be the one you bank with. Check charges and opt for the best rates. Charges are calculated in relation to your turnover and the number of debit transactions/value of credit transactions, that you accept per annum. A new business will not have this information, but shop around after you have been trading for more than a year, or if your turnover rises for any reason, and negotiate a better rate.

When accepting a credit or debit card payment you will need to run the card through your electronic machine and have the customer enter their four-digit pin number. You also need to check that:

- if the card specifies that the card holder is a Miss or Mrs, the person in front of you is female, and a male if it says Mr;
- the number and dates printed by the machine match those on the card;
- the dates on the card are valid;
- the amount printed by the machine is that being charged;
- the card has not been tampered with in any way.

If the machine picks up any problems – such as the card having been reported stolen – it will inform you what to do. If not, it will show that the transaction has been confirmed and you can move on to your next customer.

For those cards that are not Chip and Pin, you must also check that:

- the customer's signature matches that on the back of the card;
- the name on the front of the card corresponds with the signature.

The move to Chip and Pin is aimed at reducing card fraud by up to 80%, as has happened in France following the introduction of the system there in the 1990s. This should be possible because the chips are extremely hard to copy, unlike the old fashioned cards with magnetic strips. Unfortunately, liability for card fraud has also shifted from the banks to the retailers. Do not assume, therefore, that just because your machine has accepted and authorised the transaction that you will receive payment. If the bank subsequently finds out that the card was stolen it may not honour the transaction and you, the shopkeeper, will be out of pocket. If you can show that you take every precaution to prevent fraud (including making all of the above checks) you may want to challenge your bank but increasingly the odds of success are likely to be against you. To put this into perspective, I have had only one such dispute with my bank in the last seven years – which, incidentally I won.

CHOOSING A TILL

At the most basic end of operations, a market trader will typically add up transactions in his or her head and put the takings in a cash box or a money belt worn round the waist. At the top of the range, supermarkets link their till to a barcode reading system which automatically adjusts records of the

stock being held and sold, producing analysis and reports of sales, purchases and stockholdings to be compiled before making tea, cleaning the
house and putting the children to bed. If only! This kind of system is an
expensive luxury most small businesses setting up cannot afford.

What type of till?

When deciding which type of till to purchase, think about the following features.

Tills that add up

The most basic of tills needs to be able to add up the prices of the items
being sold and display this total for both the customer and shop assistant
to see. This prevents mistakes in your, or your staff's, arithmetic.

Tills with 'departments'

A more sophisticated till will allow each stock line to be entered under a
different 'department'. A fruit and veg shop might set the till up for fruit to
be entered on button number 1, vegetables on button number 2, flowers
on button number 3, and so on.

Between six and ten departments is useful. More than ten and it is difficult
to remember what each department is for. They can be used for a broad
overview of sales (all vegetables go on one button) or to monitor specific
lines (dedicate one button to pumpkins in the run up to Halloween).

Departments allow analysis of sales at the end of each trading period.

◆ EXAMPLE ◆

> If the department for fruit shows lower takings than any of the other departments,
> is it right that fruit takes up more floor space in the shop than flowers or
> vegetables which are more profitable lines of stock?

Departments can help to plan the buying and maintenance of a healthy
balance of stock.

> **◆ TIP ◆**
>
> Beware of spending too much time analysing sales data and not enough time cleaning; attractively displaying the stock already held; sourcing new lines …

Tills that operate with a till roll

This provides the customer with a receipt. This is vital if you are selling anything that may be returned to the shop for a refund, when you will need proof that the article was purchased from your shop, and the date on which it was purchased.

I have found it common for people to demand a refund for an item that has been bought from another shop; come from your shop but was never paid for (ie has been stolen); or was bought several years before.

A till roll also enables 'X' and 'Z' readings to be printed.

A 'Z' reading is printed off at the end of each trading period. This is usually the end of each day, but could be the end of the week. It gives details of total takings since the last time a Z was run off and clears the till of this information. It will give totals for the:

◆ value of sales made;
◆ number and value of cash, credit card and cheque sales;
◆ number and value of items sold by department;
◆ number of customers;
◆ value of refunds given;
◆ number of times the till has been opened other than to make a sale.

An X reading gives the same information as a Z but does not clear the till of this information. It can be used throughout the day if you want to check takings.

There are single or double till rolls. A single till roll enables you to give the customer a receipt and print off X and Z readings.

A double till roll is one till roll on top of another. The top roll will come off as a receipt to the customer whilst the second roll rewinds itself back into the till, keeping a copy of each transaction. This is very useful if you have unsupervised staff working in your shop. If you have any queries or perhaps suspect that money is going missing, it is possible to check back through every single transaction.

In summary, a simple, affordable till for a new small business will:

◆ add up;
◆ display the sale total;
◆ allow cash, cheques and credit/debit purchases to be entered separately;
◆ provide a receipt;
◆ have about eight departments;
◆ probably be a refurbished, second-hand model (approximately £100 second-hand versus £400 new).

THE FLOAT

Selling products from 50p up to £150, with many items priced at 99p or £2.99, requires a large float. I have always worked with the following amounts in the till:

£1 of 1p	£2 of 20p
£1 of 2p	£10 of 50p
£1 of 5p	£40 of £1 coins
£1 of 10p	£40 of £5 notes

with an extra £8 of 1p and £2 of 2p coins kept in the back room, to top up throughout the week. This ensures I am not rushing to the bank every five minutes for change and does not clog the till up with excess amounts of coins, which need to be counted every night when resetting the float.

Looking down on a standard till drawer, you will see the following:

£5	£10	£20	**
20p	50p	£1	*
1p	2p	5p	10p

Coins and notes are always in the same location. Notes are put in the till with the Queen's head up and to the front.

This enables staff to serve customers efficiently and accurately, and for the cashing up or checking of the till to be done quickly and correctly.

There are two sections of the till tray which are not dedicated to specific coins or notes and these are used as follows:

* As £2 coins become more common this may become dedicated to them but in the meantime I use it for the small stock record cards that are removed from items as they are sold and keep for the updating of records at a later time.

** This tray will hold any £50 notes, credit card dockets and cheques that are taken, as well as any large stock record cards, as above.

> ◆ TIP ◆
>
> When accepting money from a customer, keep it on top of the till until you have given them their change and receipt, in case they say you have shortchanged them.

SUBTLE PRICE DIFFERENCES

Most of my prices end with 99p. Some shops, including Marks & Spencer, round prices to the nearest round number: £25, £30 etc, but I find that customers view £30 as being much more expensive than £29.99. There is a psychological leap from one price to the other, which is why most shops have stuck with 99p.

Some shops finish every price with 95p. This means there is no need to hold 1ps and 2ps as part of the float. Changing from 99p to 95p is a difference of approximately 4% and although this might not seem very much, over a year's takings this will add up to a considerable amount. 4% will probably cover the business' merchant service (credit card) charges.

BEWARE OF FORGERY

This applies particularly to £20 and £50 notes. Protect yourself from such fraud by checking each note before accepting it from a customer.

- The 'Bank of England' written along the top left of the note should feel rough to the touch.
- The vertical, dotted, silver line on the left-hand side will become a solid line when held up to the light and viewed.
- The 'empty' white space in the middle of the note shows a picture of the Queen's head when held up to the light or under a UV light.
- A forgery detection pen drawn across the white space will change colour if the note is forged.

It is in your interest to make these checks. If you try to pay a forged note into the bank, or spend it in another shop, you will lose the money and have to answer questions from the police about where the note came from.

◆ TIP ◆

Keep up to date with new security measures being introduced to prevent forgeries and changes to which notes and coins are still legal tender. Ask your bank for details.

VAT

Value Added Tax, a tax added to most goods and services, is 17.5% at the present time. A quick way to work out this amount without a calculator, is to divide the net figure by 10, add on half, and add half again.

◆ EXAMPLE ◆

VAT on £40 = £7.00

10% of 40 = 4

$\frac{1}{2}$ of 4 = 2

$\frac{1}{4}$ of 2 = 1

£4 + £2 + £1 = £7.00

If your annual turnover is, or looks like it will be, equal to or greater than £60,000 (as at January 2005), you must register for the payment of VAT with Customs & Excise. This figure is set by the government and usually rises slightly each year. It is possible to register even if your turnover is less than this. Doing so will enable you to claim back the VAT on purchases you have made and may be beneficial if, for example, you are spending out large amounts of money on fitting out a new shop. This is a decision that should be discussed with your accountant to ensure you are fully aware of the implications.

All your large suppliers will charge VAT on your purchases, and in turn you will charge your customers VAT on your sales. At the end of each quarter you must add up all sales and purchases, calculate the VAT for each of these figures and pay the difference between the two VAT amounts to Customs & Excise.

◆ EXAMPLE ◆

A: Total Sales of	£117,500.00	VAT of	£17,500.00
B: Total Purchases of	£55,000.00	VAT of	£8,191.49

$$A - B = \text{VAT to pay } £9,308.51$$

In the unlikely event that VAT on purchase exceeded VAT on sales, you would be eligible for a VAT refund. This is an unusual situation and may well ring alarm bells at Customs & Excise. Avoid alarming Customs & Excise. They wield enormous powers and a VAT inspection can delve deep into all your business and personal affairs. Even if you have nothing to hide, a session with the Spanish Inquisition might be more pleasurable.

Always ensure your VAT is accounted for, and paid correctly, on time. VAT is charged quarterly and paid one month later, eg the VAT for January, February and March will be calculated and paid at the end of April. This means that when you register for VAT, there could be four months of takings before you pay what you owe. At 100% mark-up, the VAT due will amount to 7.44% of takings over that period.

It has been said that once Customs & Excise get their teeth into you they will not let go and you would be neither the first (nor the greatest offender) to be brought down by the Tax Man – remember Al Capone?

Anomalies

There are some goods that are treated differently, including:

♦ Books, newspapers, children's clothing and shoes which do not attract any VAT.
♦ Clear, unscented oil for use in lamps, attracts VAT at only 5%, as opposed to coloured or scented oil, which attracts VAT at the full 17.5%. This is because the clear, unscented oil is classed as fuel.

I have stocked both books and lamp oil at various times but have never sold either in large quantities. As a result I have always decided not to account for them differently in the VAT return – I treated them as though they were rated at 17.5%.

This results in a slightly higher VAT charge for me and the 'error' is always in Customs and Excise's favour. Calculating the exact sales of these products would take time to do. Time being money, this would cost more to calculate than I believe I would save.

6

SECURITY IN THE SHOP

SHOPLIFTING

With any luck you will be a victim of crime from the day you open your doors to the public. I say 'with any luck', because to avoid paranoia, shoplifting must be looked at as a sign of success.

- You are clearly stocking things that people want.
- Shoplifters prefer the distraction of other shoppers. Nobody will be coming in to steal, unless there are other people coming into the shop to buy.

'Shrinkage' or theft, both by the public and your own staff, is an occupational hazard and combatting it is really a question of damage limitation rather than solving the problem. It is important not to take it personally (something I find very hard to do). If you catch someone stealing from you, any form of retribution or even restraint can lead to you being dealt with more harshly by the law than the thief.

When you do see people slip something into their pocket or under a coat, you must not grab hold of them, or accuse them of having taken anything until they leave the shop. If you tackle them before, then they can say that they were about to put the item back and accuse you of making false accusations, and even assault. You can, however, make them aware you know and thus encourage them to put the item back on the shelf before leaving the shop. This is easier than having to chase someone up the street and quicker than waiting for the police to come and then give statements.

If you do catch someone, either call the police, or take the goods and tell the person to leave.

◆ EXPERIENCE ◆

On one occasion, I was working alone in the shop when an elderly lady came in with one of those shopping bags on wheels. She smiled and browsed around until some other people came into the shop. I then saw her drop several greetings cards into her bag. She looked back at me, smiling, and carried on round the shop. Some nail varnish was added to the bag and again she turned to see where I was looking. Eventually she went to leave and I made my move. Her response was pitiful, begging me not to call the police and as the value was so low, I took the goods from her and told her not to come back. The other people in the shop were all ears whilst this was happening but they seemed to appreciate the matter being dealt with in a pragmatic way. Later, I realised that there had been enough packs of meat in her bag for a small banquet and I wondered if the local supermarket had had anything stolen that morning!

On other occasions I have called the police. The results have ranged from a recorded message saying, 'The police station is closed until Monday morning. In an emergency, callers should dial 999', a ticking off for the offenders from the local beat bobby, right up to full prosecutions. These take time to get to court and you tend to forget they are happening, until a police constable comes into the shop to return the stolen items at the end of the trial.

INSURANCE REQUIREMENTS

Your insurance company will set out security criteria depending upon what you stock and the area you are in. If you stock valuable jewellery, for example, your policy will undoubtedly require full shutters over the windows. Solid, external ones are the most expensive but they protect both the stock and the glass windows.

Clothing will probably require an alarm system connected to a central monitor that automatically alerts the police should the alarm go off. The most common of these is the BT Red Care Alarm system, which involves both an installation cost and an annual maintenance agreement.

AT THE COUNTER

- ◆ If you run a shop by yourself, keep the till locked and take the key with you when you leave the counter area.
- ◆ Consider having a barrier (a rope, or a counter top) to prevent people coming round behind the counter.
- ◆ Secure charity boxes to the counter – some people have no compassion.

◆ EXPERIENCE ◆

There is a parade of shops in North London that is rather more up market than your average out of town, secondary location parade of shops. They stock designer suits, eveningwear and jewellery aimed at the local millionaires (including a high proportion of football players and their wives who live in the area). These shops have gone the extra step of having a security system on the door, which means that the customer needs to ring a buzzer for the shopkeeper to unlock the door and let the person in. Not only does this serve as additional security but discourages passing 'riff raff' from coming in to browse, enhancing a sense of exclusivity. This is not to be recommended for most shops. I want all the riff raff I can get!

◆ TIP ◆

Never leave the shop unattended, for example to go into the stockroom.

VULNERABLE AREAS

Spinners, for cards or other inexpensive, impulse buy products, can be put on the pavement outside the shop each day. They are a good way of getting people to stop, look at the shop and come in to buy. They are very vulnerable to having some of the stock (or even the whole spinner) stolen. Ensure the selling price will allow for losses or treat them as loss leaders – a line which generates sufficient sales to more than compensate for the losses.

Goods just inside the door are easy to snatch. When possible, use this display area for items that are inexpensive, bulky and difficult to move. Secure more expensive products behind glass or again, have a high profit margin to cover losses.

Where possible, group items on the shelves in such a way that you can see at a glance if any are missing.

Watch people all the time there is anyone in the shop. Make sure nothing 'falls into their bag' as they walk round the shop, or goes under their coat. It is much easier to see what is going on in summer, without all those bulky overcoats.

Clothes

When customers try clothes on, count the number of garments they take into the changing room. If unsure, check – it might look like two hangers and therefore two garments but there could be a third hanging from the clothes, hidden between the visible hangers.

Count to see that they bring out the same number they went in with.

Are they still wearing your stock under their own clothes? An empty hanger left in the changing room is a sign that something may have been stolen.

Check regularly for clothes that have fallen off their hangers onto the floor under the rails. Thieves will 'drop' things for collection later.

To prevent a handful of clothes being snatched, hang the hangers alternately, that is have one hook facing in, the next hook facing out, the third hook facing in, and so on. This is particularly important when the rail is near a door.

Jewellery

Keep expensive items in locked cabinets. Have only one item out at a time and re-lock the cabinet each time. When taking a tray of rings out of a cabinet, lock the cabinet behind you, then take the tray back to the counter and keep hold of it.

My main supplier of silver rings, a company that had retailed its own stock for many years on Camden Market, advised that I would make more money than I would lose if the rings were freely available to try on. I certainly sold more rings when they were not behind glass and could be tried on, but whether or not I was making a profit on them, I am still not sure.

◆ EXPERIENCE ◆

A policeman once brought back 32 silver rings that one young shoplifter had been caught with, having stolen them from my shop. For a while I marked up the prices more than other stock and took the losses. Eventually I developed special ring trays whereby all stock can be secured to the tray but still tried on. It is possible to steal them but not without a knife or scissors.

THEFT AND OTHER LOSSES BY STAFF

Theft by staff can be as minor as taking home a pen or as serious as helping themselves from the till.

I sell cigarette papers for 'rolling your own'. Most customers come in with the correct money and do not wait for a receipt or to have the goods put into a bag. It can be tempting for staff not to ring these sales into the till, but simply to pocket the money. A security system with a CCTV camera pointing at the till may help to deter such theft.

If you offer staff discount, check whether a member of staff is buying less than normal – if so, is it because they are getting everything they want for nothing?

Where displays of stock are put outside during the day, make sure that all members of staff are aware that it is their responsibility to bring the goods back into the shop at the end of the day – I am sure I have potentially lost more from staff going home and forgetting to bring the spinners in at night than from any amount of shoplifting during the day!

DETERRENT SYTEMS

CCTV

These systems are expensive to install. How much of a deterrent they are to both staff and customers is difficult to quantify and I have certainly never had a conviction for theft from using such a system.

One reason for this is that the whole act of stealing has to be seen clearly on the recording and inevitably the thief obscures part of the act from the camera or the camera does not quite cover the area of the shop where the action is taking place.

◆ **EXPERIENCE** ◆

A man was filmed taking an item of clothing from the rail and dropping it into his bag. He then walked out without paying. The problem was that the main part of the bag was just out of the camera shot and although we knew what he had done, there could be no prosecution because he was not stopped at the time of leaving the shop. He would have been able to argue that he had just dropped the item onto the floor and left it there even though this was certainly not the case.

Given the above, CCTV is much more effective when protecting larger items, such as furniture, and has the added benefit of detecting, and there-fore deterring, vandalism as well as theft.

Another annoying issue with CCTV is that on a number of occasions I have taken a video recording to the police and generally ended up not only out of pocket from the goods being stolen, but also from the loss of the videocassette, which the police never seem to give back.

Mirrors

Convex mirrors are available from shopfitting suppliers and can be easily installed above the heads of customers. These enable staff standing behind the counter to see into the blind spots of the shop.

Increased numbers of staff

At £5 per hour for a seven-hour day, is an extra £35 of wages going to prevent £35 (cost price before VAT) of goods leaving the shop every day? If staff are not busy all the time I find they are more likely to stand chatting, making two people less vigilant than one.

Security tagging

Mainly used for clothes, again for a small shop these systems are expensive to install. The decision to purchase such a system will depend on whether you believe the value of your goods warrants the extra expense and whether or not the tagging will be more efficient and effective at preventing theft than having extra members of staff on duty. Having more well-trained and diligent staff on the shop floor can mean improved personal service for customers and thus more opportunities to open and then close sales.

Before purchasing any such system, I recommend monitoring losses from shoplifting over a given period and then making a financial decision based on the amounts stolen. Bear in mind also that tagging systems are not foolproof. Determined or professional thieves will find ways to remove the tags, sometimes damaging the goods in the process so that even if the item is not stolen, it may not be re-saleable. They will also use lined bags and other tricks to conceal the still tagged goods, shielding them from the alarm as they leave the shop.

An audit trail

Most tills can be used with a double till roll, one copy of which is given to the customer as their receipt and the other rewound into the till. This copy can be checked to see all the transactions that have been made. Depending on the sophistication of the till, it will give such details as time of sale, method of payment and member of staff making the transaction.

When making decisions about security, prevention is better than having to deal with the emotions of being stolen from and the time spent prosecuting thieves. You will never know how much you achieve in preventing theft, but the amount you do lose is a sign of your success as a buyer.

7

STAFFING

There are four people named Everybody, Somebody, Anybody and Nobody. There was an important job to be done and Everybody was asked to do it. Everybody was sure Somebody would do it. Anybody could have done it, but Nobody did it. Somebody got angry about that because it was Everybody's job. Everybody thought Anybody could do it but Nobody realized that Everybody wouldn't do it. It ended up that Everybody blamed Somebody when Nobody did what Anybody could have done. (Anon)

Can't be bothered or don't know how to? Deliberately or accidentally? There are many reasons why people behave as they do but the key to harmony in the workplace is to employ the right people in the first instance. Wages are the greatest cost to a business but people can be a great asset if you employ the right ones. You will get it wrong at times and when you do there will be:

◆ high staff turnover;
◆ phone calls at opening time on Monday mornings, claiming illness;
◆ money missing from the till;
◆ stock disappearing;
◆ all in all, a damage limitation nightmare.

Generally speaking, it is easier to successfully recruit full-time staff rather than part-timers. With financial commitments such as rent or mortgage, they usually need the money. They tend to be older than the students who apply for part-time work, and have a better work ethic. Even so I have had an oddball bunch, complete with a long list of medical conditions and even assorted addictions, from chocolate and cigarettes to cannabis, ecstasy and who knows what else.

This is not, however, a chapter on the legalities of how to employ staff. There are many excellent books available giving the details of employment law and I would suggest buying at least one. *Employment Law Made Easy* by Melanie Slocombe (Law Pack Publishing, 2004) is in a simple, easy to read format and gives samples of letters, contacts and procedures, as well as legal requirements and rights.

This chapter is about the reality of employing staff.

RECRUITING YOUR STAFF

An advert on the shop window

This is free advertising. It will attract people who are already customers – which can lead to some quick thinking when it comes to rejections. You might not want somebody within a million miles of your shop as an employee, but would definitely not want to lose him or her as a customer.

Word of mouth

This can introduce you to excellent employees but beware of employing friends or taking recommendations from friends. It can lead to a tricky situation if the new member of staff does a runner with the takings. Employing friends of current employees generally results in too much time spent chatting and to factions within the staff team.

An advert in the local newspaper

This involves a financial cost. If you prefer, advertisements can be placed anonymously using a PO Box number, with the advantage of potentially attracting people who would not normally apply to your type of business. The disadvantage is that some people will be put off applying if they do not know what sort of business they are applying to.

Recruitment agencies

Expensive. They will charge a percentage of the first year's wages as a fee for the placement, but can act as a filter to weed out unsuitable applicants.

Job centre

There is no charge for this service so it is worth registering your vacancies with them. Particularly at times of high unemployment, however, you may receive large numbers of totally unsuitable applicants. Everyone signing on will be encouraged to apply to fulfil his or her target number of applications.

The most effective method will depend on such factors as your exact location, the time of year, whether there is high unemployment or full employment at the time you are recruiting and the particular position you are recruiting for – you would not go to a recruitment agency to find Saturday staff.

STARTING WITH AN ADVERT

Start with an advertisement in your own window, register the vacancy at the job centre and generally spread the word. If you have tried but failed to find someone suitable in this way, then place an advert in the paper.

PART–TIME SHOP ASSISTANT REQUIRED

Hours 9 am till 1 pm, Monday to Friday

Apply in writing giving details of your qualifications

and experience, together with your reasons for applying for the

job, to ...

A simple advert including the above information creates a first trawl of those who are literate and able to follow instructions.

I do not specifically ask for a CV (Curriculum Vitae) – a formal listing of your education, qualifications and work history – because I have found that many people do not know what a CV is. Many applicants for shop work, particularly the part-time positions, are still at school/college or have recently left and do not yet have much information to put on a CV. I find out more about people when they express themselves in the form of a letter.

Such an advert in the shop window will repeatedly result in people coming in to ask how to apply, what the hours are, school children asking if they can apply, and so on.

A written application will give a clue to the level of literacy, although beware that the job centre/recruitment agencies will compile CVs. If the qualifications stated are important to you then ask to see certificates – the odd 'embellishment' has been known to occur.

READING INTO AN APPLICATION

Qualifications

If someone is highly qualified, why are they applying for a lowly shop worker position? If someone has no qualifications, are they still going to have the basic skills to do the job for you? Lack of literacy and numeracy skills has been a problem with many of my potential employees and I have had to teach every Saturday worker how to calculate percentage discounts.

Work history

Have they had many jobs? How long have they lasted? If they are currently employed, why are they leaving? If they are unemployed, how long for and why?

Should any of these points flag up queries then there may be genuine reasons but you will want to question the applicant and find out more.

Once you and your business start to develop, you will be looking for a team of people who have all the strengths and skills that a strong team can provide. Tempting as it may be, it will not benefit you to recruit people who are 'in your own image' as you will be duplicating the strengths that you already have and missing out on the other skills that your business requires. The most effective team will be one that includes people fulfilling all eight of the following roles:

◆ A co-ordinator and social leader who guides but is probably not creative.
◆ A task leader to provide the energy.
◆ The ideas person. Innovative but not good at detail.
◆ An analytical person to monitor and evaluate progress.
◆ The 'fixer' who always knows someone who can help, whatever the situation.
◆ A practical organizer and administrator.
◆ A mediator who builds on the ideas of others.
◆ The progress chaser, who ensures schedules are kept.

As a one-man band you will perform all of these roles – some better than others. You will need to learn which are your strong points and which are your weaknesses. As your business grows you should try to recruit people who can contribute most where you are weakest.

CONDUCTING AN INTERVIEW

Every interview is different. Some people are chatty and volunteer all sorts of information, with others it is like drawing blood from a stone. Both scenarios tell you about the person.

The purpose of an interview is to find out as much as possible, in a limited period of time, about the person applying for the job. Ask questions that encourage people to talk about themselves and their experiences. Listen to what they say, both verbally and physically (see 'Making the Sale', page 55). Keep questions clear and to the point.

Begin the interview with questions that start with:

+ 'How did you ...?'
+ 'What happened when ...?'
+ 'Tell me about ...'

These are called open questions. They encourage the candidate to talk.

Questions that ask for a short '*Yes*' or '*No*' answer, such as '*Do you have a clean driving licence?*' are called closed questions. They are useful for checking facts but too many may make the candidate 'dry up' and stop talking.

Probing questions such as '*How would you deal with a customer who is returning a faulty purchase?*' focus on areas that you are interested in.

It is useful to have a basic structure to guide the interview.

1. Ask candidates to tell you about themselves. There is usually something on the application that is a good opener – 'I see you are a keen tennis player/have recently moved to this area/do voluntary work with the RSPCA.' If you can find an area that they are interested in then this helps them to relax, forget their nerves and be more natural.
2. Discuss their schooling (if they are young enough to remember) and qualifications and lead into asking about their employment history. Many applicants for shop work come from teenagers who are still at school/college or have recently left. A good worker will probably have had a steady Saturday job.
3. Tell them about the set up of the shop, where they will be working and with whom. If they will be working largely on their own ask how they feel about this.

When asked why they are applying for the job, many applicants reply, 'Because it would be really cool to work here'. This shows a complete lack of understanding about the reality of shop work. You should follow up by asking how the person feels about dusting, vacuuming floors, cleaning windows and mirrors, polishing silver, removing chewing gum from carpets, wiping sticky marks off counters ...

◆ TIP ◆

A shop assistant's job involves an awful lot of cleaning. It is better to be frank and put a candidate off than employ someone who will not perform the tasks of their job.

Ask what they liked about their previous jobs and what they disliked.

Ask if they have any holidays booked. This is not a bar to being offered the job but the sooner you know, the easier you can accommodate someone who can only work a week before going away for a month's holiday.

In summary:

◆ Ask mainly open questions.
◆ Ask closed questions only to confirm facts.
◆ Use probing questions sparingly.
◆ Smile, nod and encourage people to talk to you.
◆ Listen to answers without interrupting.
◆ Be relaxed and keep your body language positive.
◆ Keep the meeting focused so that you can find out which interviewee is right for the job you are offering and the interviewees can find out if the job you are offering is the right one for them.

TAKING UP REFERENCES

Ask for references from the current and next most recent employer. Be suspicious if the candidate is reluctant to do this, and wants to give a personal reference or someone other than his or her line manager. This could indicate a problem, for example there may have been disciplinary issues. If the candidate tells you why there is a problem with one of their employment references, then it is for you to decide whether that candidate is worth pursuing – up-front honesty is a good quality.

The reference needs at least to confirm the dates of employment and reason for leaving, as given by the candidate. It is useful to ask about the person's attendance record and whether the employer would re-employ/recommend the candidate as an employee. (See example of a letter asking for a reference in the appendices.)

Take up references before offering a job, or make any offer subject to satis-factory references. This gives you a get out clause if you discover the person has a history of being dismissed for gross misconduct – it does happen.

Gross misconduct is generally for theft from the employer or violent behav-iour. When running a small, cash-based business, where every member of staff is a key employee, it is vital that every employee can be trusted.

References can really only be an indication, not something to be totally relied upon as anyone with an ounce of common sense is not going to give the name of someone who will provide a bad reference. (That said, you are looking to employ people with common sense!)

◆ TIP ◆

It is far better to identify a potential employee as a problem than be stuck with them in your employ.

MANAGING YOUR STAFF

Induction and training

A sample induction sheet is shown in the appendix. Give a copy to the new staff member on their first day and keep a copy on their file. It is a useful prompt for all the things they need to be told about. I always forget to say where the toilets are and have had many a new employee standing behind the counter with their legs well and truly crossed by lunchtime on their first day!

It should list the key points the person is going to need to know for their job:

- The names of the people they are going to be working with.
- Contact telephone numbers, eg who to call if they are not well and will be unable to come to work.
- Health and safety issues, eg where the fire extinguishers are kept, how they are used, evacuation procedures, etc.
- Pieces of equipment they will be using and need to be trained on.
- Procedures that need to be explained, eg price tags are removed from items at time of sale and put in the till for stock control.
- Products that require specific knowledge, eg aromatherapy oils need an explanation of the principles of use and what each oil is used for specifically.

A general introduction should be made to all points on the first day. Specific areas can be covered in more depth over the next few weeks. It is really useful to have a staff handbook around which induction training can be focused. The handbook should cover in detail all aspects of working in the shop, the products that you sell and any procedures that are specific to the way you run your business. There should be at least one copy kept in the shop to be referred to at any time and one copy given to each employee on their first day. The clearer the instructions, the more likely the business is to run smoothly. If it is written down then nobody can say, 'I didn't know.'

MOTIVATION

Recruiting is a time consuming and, if using recruitment agencies, costly activity. Once you have found good staff you will want to hang on to them. You will also want them to contribute positively to your business. In other words you want them to be motivated. Some people would claim that they are motivated to do a job purely by economic self-interest, ie by the amount of money they are paid, but there are many rewards that affect people's performance at work, including:

1. Those provided by the employer and the work itself:
 - a monthly pay packet;
 - perks ranging from staff discount to a pension plan;
 - paid annual leave;
 - status within the workplace;
 - status in the community;
 - pleasant working conditions;
 - variety of tasks;
 - flexible working hours;
 - social contacts;
 - praise;
 - promotion.

2. Those provided internally by the employee, from having done the job well:
 - self-respect;
 - a sense of achievement;
 - a feeling of having learned something;
 - a feeling of having done something worthwhile;
 - a feeling of having made a contribution.

Areas that make people feel particularly good about their jobs include:
 - achievement;
 - responsibility;
 - advancement and a feeling of growth in job competence.

Those that make people feel particularly bad are:
 - inadequate salary;
 - poor working conditions;
 - lack of recognition;
 - lack of job security;
 - poor supervision.

Learn to delegate

People appreciate being given responsibility, and making members of staff responsible for specific areas of work will free you up to do other things. It is important, however, that both you and your employees understand what is expected of them and that your instructions are clear and specific. Working with the SMART rule will help you make this a habit. Keep tasks:

Specific
Measurable
Achievable
Realistic
Tangible.

◆ EXAMPLE ◆

When delegating the changing of the window display to a particular member of staff, be **specific** and say which window if you have more than one. Make it **measurable** by stating that it must be done every two weeks, so that you can check it has been done. Make it **achievable** by supplying all the items that will be needed to make the change. Make it **realistic** by allocating time when the person is not expected to be performing other duties. Make it **tangible**, a real and worthwhile activity that the person can take pride in doing.

When delegating, never forget that if the job is important enough to be delegated it is important enough to be supervised. In this example, that would include meeting with the designated person to discuss what the themes are going to be for each display. For an inexperienced person it would be necessary to meet before each display change to discuss exactly what is to be done and how. Once the person knows what to do the meetings can become less frequent, and cover plans for a longer period of time. Delegation of a task is not dumping it on somebody else. Keep track of what is going on and ensure that the job is being done properly.

Use positive language

Motivate others and yourself by always being positive. Get into the habit of looking for ways to make the best of life, even when everything appears to be dire. Consider the following:

'I have a problem with your attitude: you have been late three times this week'

This is a negative statement, which immediately makes the member of staff you are talking to feel defensive. It is not a good way to open a discussion about encouraging someone to improve.

'You have been late three times this week: this situation needs to change.'

This is less confrontational. The message is not positive, but provided it is not spoken in an aggressive manner, it leaves open the possibility that the matter can be discussed and resolved.

'Your sales figures have been good this month and I am very pleased with the new price labels you have made for the window display. What has happened to your time keeping, however? You have been late three times this week'.

This starts with positive feedback, making the person feel good about him or herself. It is a more effective way to discuss the need to change behaviour.

'Your sales figures have been good this month and I am very pleased with the new price labels you have made for the window display. You have an opportunity to be sales assistant of the month if you can improve your time keeping. Is there a reason why you have been late three times this week?'

This is very positive, giving the employee something to aim for and opening the discussion in a non-threatening manner, whilst looking for reasons for the lateness, which can be resolved.

Establish clear boundaries

Your employees are first and foremost there to work for you, not to be your friend. You will have far fewer disciplinary issues if you make this distinction clear from the start.

If you are male and employ female staff (or vice versa) avoid putting yourself in a potentially compromising situation, such as being alone with someone in the stockroom. Unfortunately there are people around today who would take advantage of the situation and, without cause, accuse you of touching them inappropriately. You could then find yourself in very hot water indeed.

FUNDAMENTAL RULES OF BEHAVIOUR

These apply to you and to anyone who ever works for you.

Do not stand in the shop doorway gossiping or smoking.

Do not stand behind the counter gossiping to other staff or friends.

The first will deter customers from entering the shop and the second will make them put their purchases back on the shelf and leave.

Do say hello to people when they enter the shop – this is friendly and deters shoplifters.

Do say thank you to people when they leave even if they have not bought anything – again this is friendly and people will return to a friendly shop.

Do say please when you ask for the money to be paid for a purchase and thank you when receiving payment and giving change.

Do stay calm and polite when customers make a complaint even if they are totally wrong. The saying may be that all publicity is good publicity, but an entry in the local paper for you being charged with assault is unlikely to be good for business.

Do offer staff discount (I offer 25%). This not only increases sales but is also free advertising when staff wear and demonstrate your products. It is a common occurrence to take a week's wages back from your Saturday staff when they do their shopping and I have often sold identical garments and cosmetics to customers who have seen my staff wearing what we sell.

POTENTIAL PROBLEMS

Arriving late
Working for me means arriving in plenty of time to:

◆ turn the alarm off;
◆ switch all the lights on;

- clean the floor;
- take out any rubbish;
- put the float in the till;
- take stock from the stockroom to replenish the shelves.

before turning the sign to 'open' and unlocking the door at 9.30 am, the opening time as specified on the shop window, to let the customers in.

Unfortunately, many employees think that being on time means:

- arriving at the specified opening time;
- going to the toilet;
- brushing their hair and touching up their make up;
- going to buy a coffee …

Someone even thought that going for a pre-booked, routine dental appointment at 9.30 am and coming in at 10 am – oops, sorry, forgot to get the coffee so will have to go out again to get it – before finally opening the shop doors at 10.15 am, meant coming in on time.

Telephones

This is a frequent bone of contention when people are 'working' alone. As phone bills are now itemised, it is easy to see what numbers are being dialled and when, highlighting anyone who is spending all day chatting to their friends instead of working. It is possible to rent a call-barring facility from British Telecom but this would send the wrong message to your employees. They all need to be treated as trusted members of the team as well as having the facility to make calls in order to do their jobs properly: customers need to be advised that their orders have arrived; the bank needs to be called when there are issues with the credit card machine; other members of staff need to be called when somebody calls in sick or needs to go home in an emergency.

◆ **EXPERIENCE** ◆

On one occasion the shop phone bill showed the same number being dialled repeatedly. It was happening mainly on Sundays when there is only one member of staff in the shop, so I could instantly tell who was making the calls, but the calls were being terminated as soon as they were being answered. Did I have a nuisance caller working for me or was it a lover's tiff? The answer turned out to be a bored parrot. My employee was constantly phoning her own home phone number, to set off the answer-phone. This enabled her parrot sitting at home alone to hear a recording of my employee's voice. Apparently parrots left alone all day become bored and this was an attempt to amuse her pet.

Lack of commitment

When I was a student my friends and I were desperate for all the money we could get, so were always looking for extra hours from our Saturday and holiday jobs. As an employer I now employ many students and other part-time workers, particularly at weekends and during the busy school holidays. Some people have worked for me right through their GCSE and A Levels, returning during university vacations and even afterwards, to fund gap years before starting their own careers. Others have stayed for much shorter periods of time, leaving for a variety of reasons.

◆ **EXPERIENCE** ◆

A member of staff working on her own needed to visit the toilets. Instead of locking the shop and putting a sign up to say that she would be back in a few minutes, she walked out of the shop leaving it open and unattended. Fortunately for her it was a quiet day and both the till and its contents were still there when she came back. She did see my point when I told her she no longer had a job.

Another member of staff had been getting increasingly bad at time keeping, so when she walked in at 9.40 am I said, 'You're late'. Without giving me a chance to say anything more, she stormed out of the shop without saying a word. She left taking the shop keys with her and despite repeated phone calls, refused to contact me or give them back. As a result I had to incur the expense of having all the locks changed – you do not want any former member of staff, especially an unhappy one, having access to your shop.

◆ EXPERIENCE ◆

One morning, another member of staff said that she was just nipping upstairs to the toilet. Perhaps she was offered a better job whilst she was up there, because I have never seen her since; she too left without giving notice or even saying goodbye.

Although both these employees were required to give one week's notice in writing of their intention to leave, they left without giving any notice at all. There is no recompense available to you the employer when this happens. Neither are you entitled to deduct money from wages to cover the cost of replacing keys and locks, a uniform, or any other company property unless that right is specifically stated in the contract of employment.

The employer has to give notice, or money in lieu of notice, if it is the employer who terminates the employment, unless the reason for termination is gross misconduct.

Industrial tribunals

If you are unsure about any employment legislation, most commercial insurance policies come with a free legal help-line. Follow their advice and aim to resolve any disputes with your employees amicably and quickly. More serious matters, which you are not able to resolve yourself may involve solicitors and ultimately an industrial tribunal. Provided you have followed the legal advice, your insurance company should cover your costs. Industrial tribunals are independent panels that rule on disputes between employers and employees or trade unions relating to statutory terms and conditions of employment. Issues include unfair dismissal, redundancy, equal opportunities and discrimination at work.

The panel is made up of a lawyer, a union representative and a management representative. Proceedings are meant to be informal so that in theory anyone, whether a worker, small businessperson or a large employer can present his or her own case without necessarily involving lawyers and the accompanying costs.

If for any reason you find yourself being taken to industrial tribunal, no matter what the rights and wrongs of the case, you have to think about it in a calm and detached manner. The chances are it will be cheaper, quicker and less stressful for you to settle this before it gets to tribunal. It will be cheaper to pay up to £1,000 in settlement rather than have the cost of a solicitor for one day's hearing. While you are getting stressed out with the thought of the hearing (which will probably be six months ahead) and spending time preparing the case, gathering witness statements and putting together a full defence package, you are wasting time. You could be concentrating on your business and making money. If you can settle for £1,000 or less you will have amply made that up, compared to the business you will lose whilst preparing the case, not to mention having to be closed for a day whilst you go to the hearing.

In spite of all this, and that slightly jaded feeling I get every time I have to recruit again, I have met some wonderful people. In particular I would like to thank Anna, Bob and Kirsty for their long service and maintaining my sanity over the years and Simone, whose service was not long and I wish it had been.

8

BUYING ABROAD AND IMPORTING

My favourite part of running the business is the buying, especially when I can do it somewhere hot and sunny. Flying halfway round the world to do it really is 'extreme shopping'. With cheap travel and ever more efficient communications, the choice of countries you can buy from is only restricted by whether or not you can sell what they produce.

I am not talking about big commercial operations, but the smaller craft-worker level of supplier who will be willing and able to supply a small shop in the UK with modest amounts of stock. Many people start their importing careers by taking a holiday and bringing back in their luggage a selection of goods they think they will be able to sell.

Provided you comply with Customs & Excise's limits of goods allowed into the UK this makes for an easy and enjoyable way to do business and test the water. Other than tobacco and alcohol, broadly speaking this means unlimited amounts of goods from within the EU and £145 worth of goods for your own use, including gifts and souvenirs, from other parts of the world. Everything else must be declared and any applicable duties or taxes paid on arrival in the UK. See www.hmce.gov.uk for further details.

You will probably start by buying in shops or from market stalls and paying the full price that is charged to tourists in that country. As you become more confident, you will search out the manufacturers and wholesalers who are supplying these local traders and be able to buy at better prices and in suitable quantities to make a sustainable line of stock for your shop.

From bringing things back in your suitcase or rucksack, you can go on to sending boxes back by surface mail, having a shipping company send boxes back by sea or air, and eventually having 20 or 40 foot containers packed full of goods shipped back to your warehouse (or in my case my loft and garage).

CHOOSING YOUR DESTINATIONS

The countries you buy from will obviously depend upon the exact nature of the business you intend to open. The following are a few suggestions together with reasons for or against but I will start with Bali in Indonesia because in my experience there are few small businesses that would not benefit from the choice available there. It is possible to travel to Bali, purchase enough stock to open a shop in the UK, and still have a head-start over your competition by having secured a wide variety of stock at prices well below those charged in this country.

Bali

Although my shops are predominantly ethnic in style, to think that this is all that is available in Bali would be to do a great injustice to the Balinese. There is everything from the ultra modern to classical antique. They are talented craftspeople, originally working in stone and wood to decorate their temples and carve masks for their festivities. They have now turned these skills to more commercial areas of activity and create goods that are supplied all around the world to retailers and wholesalers.

Furniture

From antique to modern minimalist; rustic to design-led; pine, oak, mahogany; leather upholstery, metalwork and stonework; all styles are available.

Interior design

There are textiles for cushions, throws and duvets, lamps and lampshades, mirrors, vases and other glassware and ceramics, from tableware to *objet d'art*.

Garden centres

Teak garden furniture, bamboo and wicker furniture for conservatories; statues and other stoneware; ceramic and terracotta garden pots from plain to highly decorative.

Leather

Quality leatherwear is on offer, including shoes and clothing, briefcases and handbags from the purely functional to designer styles.

Jewellery

They manufacture in gold, silver, semi-precious stones, costume, plastic or wooden beads. From mass production to individual pieces, buy what you see or take your own designs and have single pieces or whole collections made to order.

Clothing

From t-shirts to eveningwear, ethnic to designer styles, all are available. Buy what is there or take out your personal designs and have your own ranges made to measure. This is achievable in relatively small quantities in a way that would not be financially possible in the UK or other places.

Shop fittings

There are large ranges of glass display cases available as well as individual pieces which could be used to give your shop an identity – mirrors, carvings, statues and so on. Buy to use in your own shops, to sell to other retailers/wholesalers/galleries or even sell selective designs to the public.

Art galleries

Certain areas of Bali are renowned for their fine artists and there is a wide choice of styles of fine art and carvings, from classical Asian to modern.

Handicrafts

These range from the small, cheap trinket-style gifts found in £1 shops, through incense, candles and candleholders, drums and didgeridoos, wind chimes, statues of Native American Indians, metal CD racks, carvings of Buddha in wood or stone, to the ethnic masks and figures that I have sold in profusion.

Thailand

This is another favoured destination of mine, not only for the excellent food that is available, but also for the jewellery, clothing, leather goods, handicrafts, furniture and home furnishing textiles. As in Bali, you can buy what you see or have goods made to order.

I buy in Bangkok but Chiang Mai in the north of the country has large markets selling jewellery and the crafts of the Hill Tribe peoples.

Nepal

I have bought clothing including knitwear here, although check your goods carefully before having them sent home.

◆ EXPERIENCE ◆

I once had a selection of woollen jumpers and velvet dresses made to my own designs in Nepal. It was only when they arrived back in the UK and I was putting them onto hangers in the shop that I realised that there were a few problems. Some had one sleeve six inches longer than the other; on others, the hole for the head to go through was far too small for a standard adult head. The scary thing is, every single item sold!

Western Europe

This is clearly the closest option and with free trade between member nations, it should be relatively easy to buy from European-based suppliers (see my warning about dealing with non-UK based companies in Chapter Two).

I know people who have bought goods from French market stalls for sale in the UK. The designs were unusual compared to what was available in the UK at the time and the purchase prices were such that they were able to sell the goods through party plan and at craft fairs for a good mark-up.

Eastern Europe

In spite of all the many different product lines and wide variety of suppliers that I have dealt with over the years, I have never been involved with suppliers from Eastern Europe. I suspect that with so many of these countries joining the EU there will soon be opportunities to do so.

India

There are large ranges of products – furniture, clothing, jewellery, giftware – which are sourced in India and, on the face of it, this would seem an ideal destination. There are, however, many British family businesses working in partnership with their Indian relatives so price-wise and logistically, I believe it would be difficult to try to compete with them.

Taiwan and China

China is booming and clearly a country to be doing business with – if you can. For those who are looking to set up a substantial wholesale business then book your flights but for those who are buying largely for sale through your own retail outlets, this will not be an option. Most of the suppliers are not interested in or set up to supply on a small scale, requiring that each item be bought by the container-load.

Africa and South America

These are excellent holiday destinations and do offer the possibilities for buying goods on a small scale. From Africa you can buy a variety of handicrafts, including wooden and soapstone carvings, ethnic masks and drums. South America is well known for its silver jewellery, textiles and clothing, particularly chunky knitwear, and other handicrafts such as ceramics. Book your flight and see what you can find.

THE ADVANTAGES OF BUYING FROM BALI AND THAILAND

- Bangkok, in Thailand, is used as a hub by many airlines and so it is easy and economical to visit both Bali and Thailand in one buying trip.
- Both countries import goods from other parts of the world – Nepal, China, India, Guatemala, etc – and it is possible to buy these imported goods in affordable quantities.
- In both countries £100 spent with one supplier will secure a significant order of goods. This could put stock on your shelves equivalent to £1,000 retail price. No European supplier would take you seriously with an order this size – neither would £100 significantly fill your shelves.
- A small player can travel out to Bali, buy a 20-foot-container's worth of a wide variety of products and ship it back to Britain at an inclusive price of less than £10,000. This would set up a shop in the UK but such a purchase could not be made in Europe or China.
- Doing business out there is working in a tropical paradise, staying in some of the best hotels in the world; a far cry from a grubby industrial estate on a wet, windy British day.

As Bali and Thailand are such important sources of supply for so many small businesses, I will focus on what you need to know for stress-free travel to those destinations. When you have exhausted these destinations and want to venture further afield, try to find out how life operates in the country you are travelling to prior to your trip; this will save much time when you actually arrive. The Internet is an excellent source of information as are guidebooks and other people's experiences of a place.

WHEN TO TRAVEL

What suits you

As I trade in an English holiday resort, January is one of the most convenient times to be away from the business and gives time for the cargo to be delivered by Easter, when trade starts to pick up. That said, it is not a time when I have extra staff available for cover. The alternative for me is to travel over Easter when my Saturday staff are able to provide additional cover in the shops during the school holidays.

The weather

The climate at your destination is also a factor for consideration. Bali, for example, has a year-round average temperature of 30°C and two seasons: wet or dry. April to September is dry and the humidity is lower during these months. Thailand has different seasons in different parts of the country. Bangkok's temperature is similar to Bali's but November to April is the dry season. Easter misses the worst of the monsoons in both countries. The downside is that our Easter holiday tends to coincide with the end of the financial year in Thailand, when suppliers run down their stocks. It can also coincide with the Thai's Songkran Festival when many suppliers close for up to a week.

♦ TIP ♦

www.bbc.co.uk/weather is easy to use and provides comprehensive information about rainfall and average temperatures which may help you to decide on the timing of your trip.

Festivals

In this country, shops and other businesses will generally be closed for a maximum of one day for our festivals of Christmas, New Year and Easter. Other countries take such events much more seriously.

Bali has so many festivals that there is one going on every day somewhere on the island. The ones that bring the whole island to a standstill, however, are Galungan and Kuningan. Dates vary so check on the Internet before booking your flights.

If you value your dignity and appearance then Songkran, the Water Festival, is not a time to be in Thailand. The origins of this festival were that a few drops of water would be delicately placed upon a person as a way of washing away the old year. It is now a raucous affair when it is impossible to walk down a street without being shot at by giant water pistols and daubed with a muddy-clay. Young people drive pickup trucks with water cannons mounted on the back and in Chiang Mai in Northern Thailand, even the fire brigade and their engines are enthusiastic participants in the festivities! Many suppliers close for a week around the festival.

WHAT TO TAKE WITH YOU

◆ TIP ◆

It is important to travel light. Every kilo of weight saved will enable you to bring back another kilo of stock. Anything you can carry back will save the cost, time and risk of loss that goes with shipping goods back.

◆ EXPERIENCE ◆

One summer the 'must have' was plastic 'henna tattoo' bands. They cost pence to buy in Indonesia and were very light. The quantities I brought back (in hand-luggage, so no extra cargo costs) covered the cost of the trip to buy them. A trip which also brought back a 20-foot container of furniture, handicrafts and clothes, and a couple of rucksacks of silver jewellery. You can make time to be a tourist, relax in the sunshine and enjoy the trip abroad – all paid for by the business.

Money

I take cash with me. £6,000 fills a container of handicrafts in Bali, provides 12 to 18-months' worth of silver from Thailand and a summer's worth of dresses and sarongs. You may prefer to take travellers cheques, but exchange rates are not as good as cash. I take credit cards for additional purchases but they are not as flexible as cash and additional charges will be levied.

Books

Wherever you are going, a guidebook such as the Lonely Planet series is invaluable for information on places to stay and eat. Once you get out there, a local map can be a useful purchase.

In some countries or areas off the beaten track, where English is not commonly spoken, you will also need a phrase book.

GETTING YOURSELF THERE AND BACK

Making the booking

I book all flights and any necessary stopover accommodation through a travel company called Trailfinders. Their staff are very helpful, well travelled and knowledgeable about the destinations. Try phoning their Bristol office rather than London, as the phone lines tend to be less busy.

Choosing an airline

The most expensive flights will be with the big national airlines and on the routes offering the fewest stopovers. Do not dismiss the smaller airlines; as well as being cheaper they can offer the best service. Sometimes stopovers are inconvenient but they also offer a wonderful opportunity to see other places, to check out possible buying destinations for the next trip and offer a chance for rest and recuperation on the way so that you do not arrive completely jet-lagged.

Check the following websites to help your decision:

- www.traveljungle.co.uk is a search engine that checks fares with airlines and agents;
- www.airlinequality.com gives reviews of airlines including details of leg room.

◆ EXPERIENCE ◆

I have always found that the Eastern airlines give much better legroom in economy than the Western carriers.

Arriving home

Have someone meet you at the airport or have your car parked there. With heavy bags to carry after a long journey you want to get home quickly, not wait for public transport.

◆ EXPERIENCE ◆

I use ABC Parking as they have offers such as a night's accommodation at a Heathrow hotel together with two week's parking for the cost of the parking. This avoids nail-biting trips through rush hour traffic and the car is then parked close by in a secure car park.

ONCE YOU ARE THERE

Hotels

Large five star, international-style hotels are nice to stay in as they are ultra clean, have modern facilities such as constant hot water, air conditioning and televisions; but are completely soulless, impersonal and you could be staying anywhere.

Small, family-run hotels and guesthouses are much more interesting places to stay where you will get more of an experience of the country and its people. Some are dubiously clean and there may be cockroaches but they give you so much more opportunities to meet both the locals and other travellers from whom you can learn a great deal about products to buy and areas or specific suppliers to buy from.

Taking care

Ensure you have any required inoculations in plenty of time before you travel and be fastidious about taking your anti-malaria tablets if you should need them.

Take the simple precautions that will ensure you avoid such unnecessary illnesses as sunburn, dehydration and insect bites. When you are travelling on business you absolutely do not have time to be ill. Check www.fitfor-travel.scot.nhs.uk for comprehensive travel health advice.

Check www.fco.gov.uk for the Foreign Office's travel advice from diplomats who are local to the area.

I will stress that I have never had any problems at all wherever I have been in the Far East but it is best to have your wits about you, especially when you are carrying large sums of money. Avoid the obvious, such as being in an isolated area late at night, and keep a close eye on your bags and pockets.

If you are staying in an international five star hotel there will probably be a safe in your room. These are usually digital safes, programmable with your own code and secure to leave valuables in. In smaller hotels and guesthouses, they often offer safe deposit boxes. These will have one key for you and a different one to be kept by the hotel. Both keys are required to open the box but I have never felt they are secure enough and prefer to carry my valuables with me. Use a money belt under your clothes and take sterling in £50 notes to take up the least amount of space.

Money

Whichever country you are in you will need to change money from sterling into the local currency at various times during your stay.

In France last year I had problems finding anywhere that would change at a reasonable rate without charging extortionate commission. As most of Europe now uses the euro there is much less need for exchange facilities and not all the banks and post offices offer this service any more.

In Bali you will see signs in many of the shop windows saying 'money changer'. Do not go in there. These are the rip-off merchants. They advertise that they charge no commission but they will take your money and you will watch them count out the equivalent amount in the local currency, the Indonesian rupiah. When you walk out of the shop you will find that somehow or other they have managed to slip a couple of your Rupiah notes off the table and back into their drawer.

The only place to change money without hassle is at the bank or at the authorised money changers. You will recognise these as smart *bureau de change* offices on the main street or as small offices on the side streets where they deal only with changing money. This is where the other money changers come with their handfuls of Australian dollars, US dollars, euros, etc which they have taken off unsuspecting tourists the day before.

In Thailand you can change money at the banks or *bureau de change* kiosks in the streets and shopping malls. You will be given the correct amount of money and the rates are good. Do not change money at the big hotels, where rates will be very uncompetitive.

Watch what is happening with exchange rates. It is advisable to change money mid-week as the rate always goes down on a Friday afternoon and back up again on a Monday afternoon. I was told in Bali that this is to cover them over the weekend, in case anything should happen after the Far East markets have closed for the week. Due to the time differences, the European and American exchange markets close later than those in the Far East.

BUYING STOCK

Look around the local shops and markets to see what is available. If you are looking to buy very small quantities buy from these places. If you are looking for quantities at more competitive prices, venture into the back streets or out into the villages to find areas where they specialise in producing specific types of goods.

Sometimes you will be buying from the craftsmen themselves, or perhaps I should say the crafts-families. Production is often a family affair with mother, father and all the children involved in carving, painting and then selling whatever it is they make. It gives me a great sense of satisfaction buying from these people because you know the money is going directly to them and not some middleman or sweatshop owner.

Prices and invoices

When you go to a supplier, always ask for 'business price' which is their wholesale price for buying in bulk. You do not want to pay the price that tourists will pay for one or two pieces. A certain amount of negotiation is expected but if the final price offered is still too high then do not try and beat it down. The shopkeeper is probably not making a huge profit and your cargo costs will be the greatest expense. Instead, look to buy further up the chain of supply.

Once you have decided what to buy, the supplier will write everything down on an invoice. As this is being done, write your own list. Annotate it with whatever notes or pictures you will need to be able to recognise the items when it comes to checking them off against the real invoice on delivery back to the UK. A digital camera can come in handy here.

The invoice will then be added up and you should check the quantities, prices and the maths before finally agreeing to it. It is generally accepted to pay a 10% deposit with the balance to be paid on collection of the goods. This can very from a few days to several weeks after you have placed the order, depending on how long it is going to take to carve, stitch or paint the items you have ordered.

Clothing and other textiles

When buying goods made of fabric it is important to inspect the quality.

Check for moth holes – even if the items have just been made up for you – and look at the seams to ensure the items are not going to come apart the first time they are used. This is particularly important with items made of patchwork and for cushion covers, which need to be able to take the strain of a cushion pad being inserted.

♦ TIP ♦

I often try garments on (even if they are not my size) to get an idea of how they are cut and how they will hang.

Jewellery

For silver jewellery, only buy sterling silver, which is made from at least 92.5% pure silver. This is known as 925 silver internationally and should be hallmarked with the numbers 925. Very small pieces of jewellery may not have this hallmark, but for large pieces I will not buy unless they are clearly marked. This is because inferior silver contains higher levels of nickel which many people are allergic to, and there are strict laws governing its use (see www.teg.co.uk/nickel). Gold comes in various grades – measured in carats. The higher the number, the greater the content of gold in the metal; 9 and 18 carat are the most common in the UK.

Wooden items

When buying from somewhere in the tropics where the humidity is high, be aware that not all the wood is properly seasoned before manufacture. When transported to Europe the change in humidity can cause the wood to dry out creating splits and cracks in expensive places.

In Bali, most of the furniture is actually made in Java but is brought to Bali to be finished, so bear this in mind when ordering and setting delivery times.

GETTING YOUR GOODS HOME

There are various ways of getting your goods back.

Post them back by surface mail

Some people think they can dodge paying taxes by sending boxes of stock from the post office. The problem is that the package can take a long time to reach its destination (two months from Thailand to England) and there is no guarantee of delivery or of not being caught by Customs. Check the cost against that of one of the courier companies; there may not be much in it, making the delay and the risk not worth considering.

Carry them with you in hand luggage or the hold of the aircraft

This is the way to import jewellery. You can fit literally thousands of pounds worth of stock into a handbag and carry it with you onto the plane. There is no lead-time or extra cost for the shipping. Goods such as clothes can go into the hold, but to be secure keep jewellery with you as hand luggage.

You will need to go through the red channel and declare the goods to Customs on arrival. Any charges due must be paid before leaving the airport. Ensure you have enough cash left over from the trip or carry a credit card. (Duty on silver from Thailand is currently 2.5% but from Indonesia there is no duty as Indonesia is classed as a developing country.)

Up to £500 worth of goods, and you can clear them yourself. Above that, Customs require their forms to be filled out in code, the meanings of which they do not divulge to mere mortals like you or I so you will need an agent to do this for you. I have mine meet me at the airport. Before I fly home, I fax him copies of my invoices and re-confirm the flight times. This service costs £80 plus VAT; easy money but the hours are somewhat antisocial.

◆ TIP ◆

When buying your stock, ask the supplier to give you two copies of the invoice as Customs will keep one but they will not photocopy it for you.

Have them sent as airfreight or 'loose cargo'

Airfreight is priced by weight so only use it for things that are light or you are in a desperate hurry to get home. It is quick but expensive. Either a cargo or courier company can do this for you. A courier company will deliver the goods to your door but cargo will need to be collected from Customs & Excise's bonded warehouse at the airport. The documents you will need from your shipping company to release your goods from Customs are: invoice/packing list, air way bill, certificates of origin and export licences.

Heavy or bulky items will be sent as loose cargo, whereby they will be boxed or crated up, and when there is space put into a container and shipped back by sea. This is cheaper but can take a couple of months.

The courier companies air freight and are fast and efficient. Companies such as UPS have offices in the main buying areas. I use this method when sending clothes back from Thailand, as I do not buy in very large quantities. There will be VAT and duty to pay.

◆ TIP ◆

> Remember to send the goods to an address where there will be someone with money to pay; the boxes only take a couple of days to be delivered so may arrive back before you do.

Have your own container

Your goods will be packed into either a 20- or 40-foot container and then the whole container sea-freighted back to the UK. This can be as quick as six weeks from Indonesia and is the most cost-effective method. In 2002 I paid approximately £2,000 for this. All shipping is calculated in US dollars, so the cost becomes less when the dollar weakens against sterling.

Be very, very careful whom you use as a cargo company. Everybody's brother in Bali has a cargo company and every taxi driver will offer to take you to meet his brother. Sometimes you will never see your goods again; other times you will be lucky but the goods will arrive six months late.

Sea freight is the method to use when buying large or heavy items. By buying furniture, handicrafts and clothes, I have been able to fill every nook and cranny of a container, thus leaving no wasted space. Small carvings can be packed into a chest of drawers, handbags inside a wardrobe. The more you can pack in, the lower the cost per item for the shipping.

Mostly the goods are packed with great care. Delicate items have wooden crates built around them and shredded paper is wrapped around vulnerable parts. This does not mean to say that everything you buy will arrive home and what is sent does not necessarily arrive in one piece.

◆ **EXPERIENCE** ◆

I used to buy wooden carvings such as dragons, which have very delicate claws and horns, but I have found it is very, very rare to get any of these back in one piece. Inevitably there are also items bought and paid for, which are shown on the packing list, but are never packed into the container.

Once the container is ready to be shipped, you will need an agent in the UK to organise the container coming off the boat, clearing through Customs & Excise at the port and being delivered to you. Following the events of 11 September 2001, Customs now require every container to be x-rayed before it is cleared (at your expense of course) and should the x-ray machine not be working, you will also be liable for the storage charges until it is fixed.

SHIPPING THE GOODS

Before leaving the UK

I fax or e-mail my cargo company before leaving the UK to tell them when I am coming out, what size of container I will need and when I am looking to send it. It is better to communicate this way, rather than by phone, as it reduces any misunderstandings due to language differences. Also, when you return to the UK, tired and jet-lagged, you will not appreciate telephone calls in the early hours of the morning. Bali, for example, is eight hours ahead of GMT and they will be calling you during their office hours.

They will quote current shipping rates but if there is a delay and the shipment is sent later, the amount can change. The US dollar exchange rate affects shipping rates, as does the political situation.

Paying and collection

Visit your cargo company on arrival in the country to advise them that you are there and once you have finished buying, go back to them with all your invoices. They should photocopy them and give you back the originals. The invoice totals will be added up and the balance to pay calculated. I pay this to my cargo company and arrange for them to collect and pay the balance owing to each supplier. They will then pack my goods and contact me back in the UK to advise on the size of container being sent and confirm how much it will all cost.

If you want cargo to pay the balance on the goods and you give them cash, there are no extra charges. A credit card payment will involve a 3.5% fee for that transaction and as the money will be going into your cargo company's bank account, there will be an additional charge for each cheque paid out to your suppliers.

You will not need to pay the actual shipping costs until you are back in the UK. Once they have collected your goods, they will wrap and pack them into a container (or two!). Some cargo companies stack the goods up in their warehouse as though they were in a container to plan the most space efficient packing – quite a sight to see.

Some buyers prefer not to come back to the UK until they have gone with the cargo company to supervise the collection of goods and overseen the packing of their container. By coming home before this is done, I risk goods not being collected correctly and the container not being efficiently packed, but for me being away from my business in England for six to eight weeks or more is too long. I do not have sufficient staff to provide cover for this period and I would risk losing more money than I would save by staying away to supervising the shipment.

The documentation

Once packed, they will contact you with a copy of the invoice/packing list.

Check the invoice/packing list carefully and list what is missing. It will probably take several communications between you and your cargo company before you are happy that everything is included on this documentation. It is important to get this right as it forms part of the importation documentation that goes to Customs & Excise.

◆ EXPERIENCE ◆

This can be an interesting document to translate. This is one for some goods I had ordered from Bali:

The document said	The item was
wooden dram 25	25 cm wooden drum
bamboo dijuridu antik	bamboo didgeridoo, antique finish
krismes tree galld	christmas tree, gold
pinguin double	two wooden penguins
jiraf 3	3 metre tall giraffe
cat duduk	some sort of cat
coki coki ekor mawar	any suggestions are welcome for this one!

Having agreed the documentation, cargo will fax or e-mail you copies of the invoice for packing, fumigating and shipping the container, together with any other charges that are due, against which you will need to make a bank transfer of funds to them. Once your cargo company has received the money, they will courier to you by air the original invoice/packing list, bill of lading, certificate of origin and export licences. You need these documents to release the goods at your end.

Fumigation and other charges

In Bali, once the cargo is packed into a container it is fumigated to kill off all the creepy crawlies and other nasty creatures that might be in there. This is a legal requirement and a reputable cargo company will do this. Other companies will take your money and when you finally open the container back home, you will have to avoid the spiders and possibly even rats that come crawling, jumping and slithering out as you unpack.

◆ TIP ◆

Depending on what you have bought and where from, there may be other charges for duties and tariffs to be paid to the government of the country you are buying from.

◆ EXPERIENCE ◆

From Indonesia, I have been charged an export tariff of US$2 per dozen trousers being exported to the UK, but no charge has been made for exporting dresses. This is a small sum to pay but it is annoying if you have included small samples of several different types of item and been charged for each type.

Clearing Customs in the UK

To avoid a complicated and time-consuming exercise, use an agent to do this for you and organise the process as early as possible. This particularly applies to air-freighted goods which only take a couple of days to arrive, and once in Customs & Excise's bonded warehouse in the UK you have a maximum of 48 hours to clear the goods before a daily storage charge is imposed.

Do not be tempted to omit items from the invoice and think you can get away without paying duty. If Customs Officers decide to open your packages and find something that has not been declared they will not simply charge you for the extra – you will lose the goods.

9

DEVELOPING YOUR BUSINESS

WHAT NEXT?

When you take the plunge to become self-employed, your life changes forever. The narrow confines of working for a major corporation or a public service provider fall away. The world is your oyster and you can make of it what you will. Being self-employed is neither a job nor a career – it is a lifestyle.

Your range of interest broadens. World stock market and currency fluctuations make you prick up your ears more quickly than the football scores. You search the Internet for suppliers in Beijing, descriptions of obscure gods and goddesses, or to read the Jakarta Post and Straits Times newspapers on-line. Thoughts of holidays are no longer to the Costa del

Suntan. The demands of your kids (or those of your friends) are less tiresome and instead become market research – it takes all members of the family to run a business.

When running a business like mine, you learn from the laws of feng shui that the seat and lid of your toilet must never be left up and that a statue of Buddha must always be introduced to his surroundings. Candles are not just something to provide light, but come in vegetarian and non-vegetarian forms. Either way, they burn for longer if kept in the freezer before use. A good nightlight candle will burn for eight hours and a standard length incense stick for 15 minutes.

Clothes made of crinkle rayon will shrink when washed, but can easily be pulled back into shape. You can interpret Tarot cards – the Fool representing the innocent youth beginning his journey in life, with his knapsack on his back and barely a care in the world – but never quite learn how to construct a new display stand without leaving out that first, vital piece.

You will wish you had a pound for every light bulb you have replaced and become an expert in amusing fractious children, to give their parents time to make major purchases.

If you have an interest in politics or a desire to change things in your locality, then being a businessperson gives you an instant foot in the door of the local chamber of commerce, business forums and breakfast clubs, with links to local councils and government.

This is a time when many employed people are living in cloud cuckoo land. They load themselves up with massive debts and fail to appreciate how little job security there is nowadays. Becoming self-employed means moving out of your comfort zone and taking risks but you quickly learn that your destiny is in your own hands; you can work to create your own security.

Having established your first shop, it is time to think to the future and consider that comfort zone again.

- Are you getting too comfortable?
- Is it time to take on the next challenge?

Even if you decide to take on the challenge of retirement, you may need to renew the shop lease to secure the sale of the business. What a waste to close down a thriving business when it could provide you with the ultimate in profitable sales!

RENEWING THE LEASE

I suppose it is possible that some landlords and tenants discuss, negotiate and come to an agreement quickly and amicably. They have their solicitors draw up or look over the new lease, then sign and carry on as before but this is not my experience.

There are many different types of landlord, from the little old lady whose family has always owned that parade of shops to professional companies who specialise in owning and managing commercial property all over the country. My main experience is of a remote landlord – an investment company – which has delegated all responsibility for the property to a large managing agent, the sort of company that would manage Blue Water Shopping Centre or the Canary Wharf office complex. Suffice to say, a managing agent that is not interested in spending time on a small development of independent retail units in a backwater well away from the metropolis. In other words, precisely the sort of place most small, independent retailers can afford.

> ◆ TIP ◆
>
> The legal position is archaic and the burden of responsibility is on you, the tenant, to maintain your right to be in the property.

The process goes as follows:

1. Not earlier than two years, but not later than six months before the tenancy is due to expire, your landlord can serve an LT9: notice by landlord requiring information about occupation and sub-tenancies of business premises, under section 40 (1) of the Landlord and Tenant Act 1954.

This is straightforward but must be replied to within one month of being served. They will also serve an LT1: landlord's notice to terminate business tenancy under section 25 of the same act. This will be served even though the landlord is telling you your lease renewal will not be opposed. This notice must be replied to within two months of being served.

2. If a new lease is not signed within four months of LT1 being served, you must apply to the county court for a new tenancy. The time limits are very important, as you will lose your right to apply to the court if you do not keep to them. In 2002, the court fee for this was £120 and the solicitor's fee for serving the court notice approximately £200.

It is generally in the landlord's and the tenant's best interest to come to a mutual agreement themselves regarding the renewal of the lease. With this in mind, the application to the court will usually result in the defendant (the landlord, if you the tenant make the court application) requesting a three-month stay (an adjournment) to facilitate negotiations between the parties. If this is agreed to, it is important to instigate negotiations as quickly as possible.

You, the tenant, will need to keep going back to court before the end of each stay to keep your rights open. Keep negotiations going to bring the matter to conclusion as soon as possible and thus keep costs down.

The government issues a booklet *Business Leases and Security of Tenure* available from the Department of the Environment. This explains the main provisions of part II of the 1954 act, but unless you are a solicitor specialising in this field, seek professional advice.

EXPANSION

◆ **Horizontal expansion** is growing what you already do. If you sell clothes, could you also sell shoes, hats, bags or other accessories? If you have one retail outlet, why not open a chain of stores? Develop an Internet site or mail order catalogue.

◆ **Vertical expansion** is developing a retail operation into a manufacturing and/or wholesale operation as well.

MAIL ORDER FROM THE INTERNET OR A CATALOGUE

Internet trading has not been the instant success that many claimed it would be. Of those companies that are purely Internet traders, Amazon is a very successful example but many have struggled. Trading off the back of a bricks and mortar business (one that has a traditional shop behind it) can be a smart move.

The main problem with an Internet business is getting your name known. Companies have gone bankrupt having spent thousands, if not millions, of pounds trying to ensure that theirs is the name that comes out on top with the various search engines. As a shop and retail Internet trader, you are better off ensuring that all your customers, and everybody who passes your shop, knows your Internet address. Have it printed on your carrier bags, sign-written on the front of the shop, even hand out fliers.

The important point when building a mail order business is to ensure good customer service; the correct items should be delivered promptly, undamaged and preferably within a stated time. This is particularly important coming up to Christmas, when many purchases are required in time for a certain day.

BECOMING A WHOLESALER

As an importer of goods it is easy to 'piggy-back' off your own stock to sell to other retailers – that is, to sell wholesale what you have imported and have in stock for your own retail use. This is a good point from which to start because you know which lines sell well and have established your supply chain.

The principles of wholesale are very much the same as for retailing. Having established which goods you are going to wholesale you will need to decide what sort of business it should be: will your customers come to you, or will you go to them? If you are operating from the back room of your shop it will probably not be convenient or appropriate to have wholesale buyers coming into the shop to place orders whilst you are trying to serve your retail customers. On the other hand, a large warehouse facility with ample parking space is crying out for cash and carry customers.

A CASH AND CARRY WAREHOUSE

The feasibility of this will depend on such things as where you are located; a warehouse in the Orkneys or Scilly Isles will inevitably be visited by far fewer buyers than one surrounded by other wholesalers in one of the country's major conurbations. The best locations are

◆ near to major arterial roads
◆ close to public transport links
◆ in the vicinity of other wholesale suppliers whom your buyers may also visit.

Opening hours

A cash and carry warehouse needs to have set opening hours. Whatever you advertise you must adhere to. Customers become very frustrated if they come to you first thing in the morning and you are not open. If I phone in advance, several of the wholesalers I use will open up early especially for me, which is a great help to me and no inconvenience to them.

◆ TIP ◆

Until you are generating enough business to justify having the warehouse open on a regular basis, operate by appointment only.

Pricing

As in your shop, the cash and carry should have goods clearly marked with prices, particularly if you offer price breaks for different quantities purchased.

Buyers prefer the simplest and most straightforward pricing policies such as one price for each item and a discount on the total value spent rather than on quantities of each item. 5% discount on £500 spent; 10% discount on £1,000 spent, is easy to understand and remember, as well as being a persuasive argument for always spending at least £1,000.

5% discount if you buy a dozen of this, 10% if you buy two dozen of that, 15% if you buy ten of something else, is confusing and difficult to remember. If every stock line in the warehouse is not clearly labelled, the customer will not know whether there is a discount or not. Such as system leads to frustration and an alternative supplier being sought, rather than greater quantities of goods sold.

Keeping staff busy

If you are employing someone to work in the warehouse, there can be long periods of the day when there are no customers to serve, no stock to shift and you may be paying them to read the papers or phone their friends (thus blocking the calls of genuine customers). Staff can be kept usefully occupied during these times by packaging some of your own products or doing some basic component work. This can be as simple as stringing beads together to make necklaces or producing information cards and attaching them to your products (see Display, page 67). Put your own logo on them and create your own brand.

Facilities

Customers often have to travel a long way when they go wholesaling, so have clean, decent toilet facilities for them to use. These will be very welcome, as will offers of coffee.

TAKING YOUR PRODUCTS TO THE CUSTOMERS

There are several ways of doing this:

◆ selling door to door;
◆ exhibiting at trade shows or fairs;
◆ mail order from a catalogue or the Internet.

SELLING DOOR TO DOOR

Another way to start as a wholesaler is to visit a town you would like to supply to and hoof it up and down the streets. Find the shop you think will best sell your stock, go in and ask for the proprietor or manager. There may be no one available to see you. If not, leave pictures and a price list in a sealed envelope, ask whom you need to speak to and telephone later to find out if they are interested. Then you can arrange an appointment for them to see more and hopefully this will lead to a definite order.

Expanding on that, you can actually take your products with you. There are two ways of doing this:

1. Take one example of everything you sell, put it in the back of a van, and drive the van to your customers. You can then write an order and send it out from your warehouse.

♦ EXPERIENCE ♦

One of my suppliers does this very professionally. The van driver phones up once a month (more frequently in the lead up to Christmas) to make an appointment to see each retailer in his area. The van is kitted out with drawers for the small items. Large items are hung on the walls or stacked on the shelf above the cab. Everything is held in place, mainly by elasticated cord and there is even a heater in the back so it is cosy in winter. He takes the orders and passes them on to the central warehouse for dispatch. This company sells many wind chimes so there is always a cacophony of noise coming from the van which must make passers-by wonder what on earth is going on inside.

---

2. Load the van to capacity with everything you sell, stocking it proportionally with what you sell most of. Drive the van to your customers, who can then buy from the selection you have and take the stock there and then.

This works particularly well for items of furniture, which are bulky to send by normal delivery routes, and for one-off pieces. Book appointments with your existing customers, but look round other towns for new places to sell on the way. If you can meet a potential new customer, they may be persuaded to take a sample selection and you can add them to your list for a proper delivery next trip.

You can visit potential customers yourself or employ the services of a sales rep or agent. Either way, the following guidelines for being a good salesperson should be followed:

- **Make an appointment** to see your customers rather than just turning up in their shops. This is courteous and can save you a wasted journey.
- **Be flexible** about the hours you work. If a retailer runs the business alone it will be better to meet outside of shop opening hours when that buyer can concentrate on placing the order rather than running the shop. This leads to bigger, more lucrative orders!
- **If you have a catalogue,** provide a price list to go with it. If you offer discounts for quantities then say so, and you can discuss this on an individual basis with each buyer.
- **Provide a supply of order forms** so that repeat orders can be placed between visits.
- **Know the goods** that you are selling:
  - what things look like (be able to provide pictures or samples);
  - the range of sizes available;
  - how items work;
  - the range of colours they come in;
  - the required order quantities;
  - whether new items are in stock yet and if not, when they are due;
  - what the expected delivery time will be;
- **Be prompt** about finding out the answer to any other questions.
- **Be discreet about prices** in front of a retailer's customers.
- **Be able to advise** what other retailers are buying and which are the slow selling lines.
- **Keep records** of what each shop has bought and follow up for repeat orders.

Provide stock on a trial basis

When you have a new product that you know will sell well, put your money where your mouth is and put a display into a shop on a trial basis. If it sells, the retailer will buy, re-order and may even exchange it for a larger display – I have certainly done so. You will also gain much credibility for the future. This can be done by providing an invoice for 60 days instead of the usual 30, with the option to settle up and return any unsold goods after 30 days.

Get your products into the best location in each town and nurture your relationship with that business. (See 'Sole trading rights', page 180)

Once you have taken the order, deal with it promptly and ensure the goods are dispatched as quickly as possible.

Sale or return

To get a foot in the door, you may consider offering to supply some shops on a sale or return basis, whereby you supply goods to a retailer without receiving payment. At the end of each month the retailer will pay you for what has been sold. Hopefully the experiment will be a success and the retailer will be prepared to buy from you. Sale or return is done on a commission basis, where the retailer will make only 10 or 20% from the sale price, as opposed to 50% from having bought the goods wholesale.

EXHIBITING AT TRADE SHOWS AND FAIRS

Stands at the big trade exhibitions are expensive and when business is booming they are often fully booked by regular exhibitors, with new people being put on a waiting list.

The success of an exhibition cannot be measured only in terms of the number of orders taken at the show. Some buyers will come back to you to place orders in the following months and you should be able to convert some of the prospective leads into orders at a later date. However, in order to maximise your return:

- **Be on the stand first thing in the morning** and ensure that someone is there until the end of the day – buyers do place orders at all times of the day.
- **Make friends with the exhibitors next to you** and cover for each other. If you are exhibiting alone, you will probably be in an area of the exhibition hall where there are other small business people also exhibiting alone. There will be times during the day when you need to leave the stand. If your neighbours can at least give out price lists in your absence this will help your potential customers and maybe keep them there until you return to clinch the deal.

- **Have prices clearly marked on the goods** so that whoever is on the stand does not have to search for a price list or ask someone else. It is so much more professional.
- **Consider sharing a trade stand with another supplier,** whose products compliment yours, to split the cost.

After the exhibition has finished, you may feel you have earned a break, but now the work really begins!

- **Deal with orders promptly** and send out the goods as quickly as you can.
- **When people have asked for further information,** get it to them as quickly as possible – it may result in another order.
- **If you are still out of stock** of many of the items that have been ordered a month after the show has ended, send what you have and put the rest on back-order. The customer can then start to sell and the back-ordered items can be sent out with the re-orders.
- **Follow up all the contacts** you have made and pursue repeat orders.

SELLING THROUGH MAIL ORDER AND CATALOGUES

For mail order companies a catalogue is a must, either as a paper copy or on-line (see pages 3 and 171). For other wholesalers, it is still very useful from a retailer's perspective if they can supply a catalogue. Some sales reps will only visit once a year and if it is a long time between visits/trade shows it is not easy to place repeat orders or expand the range. This is particularly true for jewellery when you are ordering a large variety of items, many of which are very similar.

◆ TIP ◆

A catalogue makes it quick and easy to find specific items, either to order or to show to a customer.

The catalogue needs to be set out logically to be useful, and depending on what you sell, it may be beneficial to produce two copies of the same catalogue. One with the wholesale prices on for the retailer's use, and the other without any prices for the retailer to mark up with his or her own retail prices to show to customers.

A number of companies do not produce a catalogue, usually because they say that their stock changes too quickly. A colour catalogue is expensive to produce and to post to enquirers who may not place an order, but with digital cameras and web sites this need not be so; a catalogue can be produced gradually, individual pages can be sent out or customers can print it themselves. As a buyer I spend far more money with companies that have catalogues than those that do not, and for some product lines will reject a potential supplier because there is no catalogue.

Breakages, short deliveries and faulty goods

As a supplier, you will know from the number of companies telephoning whether there is a genuine problem with your packing and/or delivery company. If there is, send credit notes out swiftly and with good grace.

If there are reports of breakages or problem deliveries, trust that the customer is not making a false claim. In my experience, even the best of suppliers and delivery companies have the occasional off day.

Invoices

A really good wholesaler will provide an invoice that fully itemises everything the retailer has bought, with all items in alphabetical or numerical order.

Small or similar items should be delivered in numbered bags with the item code or other identifier clearly marked. All other products should be clearly identifiable by the description on the invoice or the code on the box they are in. This makes checking off an invoice quick and accurate – a plus point your company will be remembered for.

Such an invoice can be used as a ready prepared stock list to keep track of what stock is held and encourages re-ordering.

RECEIVING PAYMENT

Cash and carry is just that: the customer pays cash and carries the goods away. As a mail order wholesaler you will need to decide how you are going to receive payment.

◆ **Pro forma**

This is the standard way to treat a new customer. The customer places the order, you raise the invoice and once payment is received and cleared, you send out the goods. This ensures payment but takes time.

◆ **Payment with order**

Some suppliers do this to ensure payment but as a retailer I do not like sending a cheque only to receive a delivery that is far short of what I have ordered and paid for. This is good for the wholesaler, who keeps the remaining money on account.

◆ **30-day invoices**

The retailer orders the goods and you send them out with an invoice to be paid in 30 days' time. The retailer has a month to earn the money to pay the invoice but you are working on credit and have no sure way of knowing that the invoice will be paid.

◆ **Using a factoring service**

You issue invoices to retailers in the normal way. The retailers pay the factoring company, who guarantees to pay you irrespective of whether or not they receive payment. Charges depend on your turnover so check out Internet sites such as gfpsurvey.cwc.net for further information.

ADVERTISING

For all wholesale businesses this is an important way to contact potential customers, as advertising is your 'shop window'. This can be done in trade magazines and mail shots.

◆ **Trade magazines**

Regular adverts should pick up new business throughout the year, unless your product is particularly seasonal. Magazines like *The Trader* are given away free at the trade shows, giving increased circulation during these months.

◆ **Mail shots**

Post or e-mail a sheet of pictures representative of the goods you sell to companies you hope to supply to (they can be line drawings or photographs). Include prices, dimensions and colours where appropriate. If you offer reductions for quantity, say so. Anyone who is interested will call you for more details. You should follow the mail shot up with a telephone call to offer more information.

◆ TIP ◆

Digital cameras and e-mail facilities make it easy to contact new and existing customers and keep them up to date with regular mail shots of new stock.

Get out and about

As a wholesaler, you should get out and about regularly to see how your customers sell your goods. Look also at what other goods your customers stock. See how much floor area a retailer devotes to your goods in relation to the rest of their shop and how prominently they display them. Are you selling a rising star? If not, you need to source new products to sell.

Find out what your customers think about the agents or reps you employ, and what sort of job they are really doing in promoting your company.

Sole trading rights

In a small town, most retailers will want sole trading rights for distinctive lines. It is then worth them making extra effort to give the product prime space and maximum promotion. If the shop next door starts to sell exactly the same product from the same manufacturer, there is a risk that both shops will downgrade the priority of the product or get into a price war to attract the greatest number of customers. This can demean the product. If neither supplier is making a decent profit from the product they may both cease to stock it. In the meantime, customers will have come to expect the lower prices from all suppliers and the product will be harder for everyone to sell.

In a large town there will be space for more than one stockist, but again they should not be in direct competition with each other.

When you offer a retailer sole trading rights in a town then stick to the agreement. If that retailer finds that you are supplying to their nearest competitor, they will find a new supplier.

SELLING THE BUSINESS

Alternatively, maybe you have had enough and feel you want to sell so you can have that well-earned break known as retirement. When it comes to selling a small business, such as a shop, it is often easier said than done. There are business transfer agents (the business equivalent of an estate agent) who will put you on their books and send out mail shots to people who have made enquiries about buying such a business. They will advertise in places like *Dalton's Weekly*, but they will tell you themselves that their filing cabinets are full of businesses whose owners would like to sell.

Why are there so many?

- **Sometimes the sellers are not sure whether or not they want to sell** – after all the business is still earning them an income and can they really afford to?
- **Others have unrealistic expectations** of what the business can sell for.
- **Yet more have books that do not show a good enough profit** to encourage anyone to buy the business.

Having said that, many people do sell businesses for a healthy profit.

Can I afford to sell?
Valuing the business
When selling a house it is fairly easy to assess what the value will be; if your house is of the same design as those in the street it will be worth a similar amount, give or take a few thousand pounds for a new kitchen, bathroom or conservatory. There will also be many estate agents in the town, all of whom more than willing to tell you what they can sell it for.

With small retail businesses, however, there are few that can be directly compared with another to give a true market value. There is no hard and fast method for valuing a business. www.bizhelp24.com advise that there are over 20 different ways to value a business. These include the following 'rule of thumb' valuations from *The 2001 Business Reference Guide* (Business Brokerage Press):

book stores	15% of annual sales + sav (stock at valuation)
florists	34% of annual sales + sav
food/gourmet shops	20% of annual sales + sav
furniture	15%–25% of annual sales + sav
gift and card shops	32%–40% of annual sales + sav
sporting goods	30% of annual sales + sav

As books, furniture, gifts and cards are just a few of the things that I sell, it begins to show how difficult and subjective it is to value a business. At the end of the day, businesses are sold for what the purchaser can afford to pay and the seller is willing to accept. If someone is offering to give you a reasonable sum of money and you really want to move on and do something different with your life, only you can decide if it is worth hanging on in the hope that someone will offer you more.

Valuing the stock

This is a more exact science. A valuation will be done at the time of handover and the stock will be valued at cost price (what it was bought for, not what it is marked up to sell for), excluding VAT. Decide whether you and the seller will do the stock-take yourselves, or if you are going to employ a stock-taker and split the cost of this between you.

It will be necessary to agree exactly how items are to be valued.

♦ **At cost price,** meaning that every item must be looked up in the supplier's catalogue or invoice to find the exact price. This would be ideal but not every item in my shop can be identified in this way. It is also a very time-consuming method and so a certain level of honesty is required from the seller in declaring what the purchase price was/what the mark up is.

♦ **As a calculation from the selling price,** eg if you always mark everything up double you can go round the shop dividing every price by 2.35 to calculate the purchase price excluding VAT.

- **Using an average price**, where you have many small, similar items that have been bought at very similar prices.
- **At a reduced price** for shop-soiled or old stock.

Whatever method you use, and it may be necessary to use a mixture, this should be discussed and agreed before the day of the stock-take. If you are counting the stock at the end of your last day's trading, so that the new owners can start trading at 9.00 am the following morning, it may be late into the night before you finish and arguing about prices will not help.

The money for the value of the stock is paid to you in addition to the agreed sale price of the business.

People who buy businesses

Selling a business is like selling a house – many people will enquire out of curiosity rather than any actual intention of buying. Others will enquire when all they really want is to find out information and use it to set up a business from scratch.

I wish I had a pound for every time someone had said to me, 'If I win the lottery I'll buy everything in this shop – in fact I'll buy the shop!' I would not need to win the lottery if I had!

Word of mouth can be a good way of advertising the business for sale. Look round your own staff team and there may well be someone who would be interested in taking on the business. It is not uncommon to have staff buy out the management. By forming a partnership or co-operative it is easier for them to raise the necessary funds.

Alternatively there are your Saturday staff, who as students are usually coming to the end of their education and need to look for a job or a career. If you are really lucky then perhaps one will have parents who are in the market for a change of career or lifestyle for themselves or simply wish to ensure future employment for their son or daughter.

When the economy is booming, company profit shares and bonus schemes provide people with the capital to change their lifestyle and buy a business. A downturn in the economy provides redundancy payments to start that new life by buying a business. There is opportunity in every scenario.

The advantage of selling to a member of staff, particularly if they have worked for you for a number of years, is that they know about your business. They will know what you sell, how the shop runs, what your takings are, and have a feel for whether or not the business is sound and if you are making good money from it. They will know which lines are selling best and whether the business is on the up or has taken a down turn.

If someone does want to buy the business from you but cannot raise the full amount of money that you have agreed, consider deferred consideration. In this way they will owe you the balance of the money, to be paid off in a manner to be agreed between yourselves. This is not ideal but provided the amount deferred is only a small portion of the sale price, it will enable the sale to go through and for you to move on to your next project. So long as you know the business is sound, you should get all your money back.

Whatever you do – good luck! And most importantly, enjoy yourself.

10

TOP TEN TIPS IN RETAIL

1. Choose The Right Location

Wait and find the right location. Do not grab the first one that is available – it may be a terminal location (see Chapter One), not a secondary one!

2. Keep Costs Low

Keep the business cash positive. Do not take on unnecessary debts (for fancy cars and the like). If you have access to an alternative income, keep it going until the business is financially secure.

3. Be Unique

Offer your customers something they cannot get elsewhere.

4. Keep Stock Changing Over

Ideally customers buy everything and ensure a steady turnover. Realistically there will be slow selling lines that must be sold off regularly, at a discount. Only new stock can maintain customers' interest.

5. Be Commercial

When buying for the business you are buying to accommodate other people's tastes. The profits of the business can be spent on what is your own taste.

6. Be Resourceful

Learn to think laterally. Look for alternative and imaginative approaches to everything, from resolving situations to displaying stock.

7. Be Competitive

Regularly review suppliers' prices and services. Buying at the best prices enables you to pass on savings to your customers and stay ahead of your competition.

8. Know Your Business

The better records you have of what has been bought and what has been sold, the better your buying will be. This increases sales.

9. Choose Staff Carefully

At their best they can make money for you, but they can lose money even faster, by discouraging customers, being lax about security, helping themselves from the till ...

10. Never Rest on Your Laurels

You are only as good as your last sale and must always be looking out for the next trend.

APPENDICES

GOAL SETTING

Most people do not know what they want to achieve in life. Others think they do but in reality there are extreme divergences between what they say they want and what they are prepared to do. Example, 'I want to be a chef in my own restaurant. I want seven weeks' holiday every year, with weekends off to go windsurfing. I want to be home by 6.00 pm every evening to play with the children before putting them to bed.' Need I say more?

Use the following exercise to establish your priorities in life. You may find self-employment is not for you but that discovery will save you a substantial investment of time and money.

Take 30 to 45 minutes over this activity. The following questions will help in clarifying your values, capacities and goals. You should answer the questions briskly, allowing no more than two minutes for each.

1. If you knew you only had six months to live, how would you live until then?

2. What are the five most important values or commitments in your life?

3. What things have given you the greatest feeling of satisfaction and importance?

4. What activity(ies) holds your interest and attention most strongly? What do you find completely absorbing?

5. What are your three most important goals in life?

6. What would you attempt if it were certain you would not fail?

7. How would you like things to develop for you over the next five years?

8. List two or three things that you really want in the spaces below (spend no more than two minutes per space).

	I want to do	I want to be	I want to have
Personal			
Work and career			
Family/relationships			

Now, spend five to ten minutes making notes on what your answers tell you. Questions 3 and 4 are pointers to your special capacities. The remaining questions are all aimed at values or aspirations. Do not be surprised by some inconsistency (which may be useful in indicating discrepancies between who you like to think you are and what you are really like) but look for the common ground between wants and values.

Finally, spend five to ten minutes formulating a substantial but credible goal that you will aim for over the next three to five years. It must be specific; it must use your special capacities; there must be things you can do that will make its achievement much more likely; you should really want it. Test your possible goals by considering the activities you will have to undertake and/or cut back on in order to achieve it, and whether you are willing to make these changes.

It helps to come back to this activity from time to time – your answers are bound to change and develop. It is a common and useful outcome for people to discover that they need to do more work in this area (because they do not know what they really want in life). Most people do not set personal goals, they think it odd, pretentious, a sign of rampant ambition … Most people do not achieve their full potential in life.

SOLE TRADER BUSINESS PLAN

1. Your personal details
   - name
   - address
   - telephone number
   - e-mail address

2. Your business name and format of business (sole trader/partnership/ limited company)

3. Type of business
   - List the products/services you intend to offer.

4. Aims and objectives
   - Personal/business aims for the next five years (eg to open a chain of four shops).
   - Objectives (eg to save £250,000 to retire in 15 years time).

5. Your business background
   - training and qualifications
   - skills and experience

6. Contingency plans
   - Brief details of your health.
   - What will happen if you are sick/injured?
   - Family support.

7. Market research
   - What is your market? Potentially how big is it?
   - Who is your customer: age, social class, income group, etc?
   - Who and where are your suppliers?
   - What are the costs?
   - What will your pricing be?
   - What laws, regulations and licenses will affect you?
   - What is the lifecycle of the product/service?
   - How will you develop the product/service?

8. Competition
   - Who is it?
   - What are their strengths and weaknesses (SWOT analysis)?

9. Unique Selling Point (USP)
   - What makes your product/service different from the competition?

10. Finance
    - income needed to survive
    - initial investment
    - working capital
    - cashflow
    - profitability
    - invoicing/bad debts

11. Marketing
    - advertising/promotions/contacts

12. Premises and equipment
    - leasehold/freehold
    - change of use
    - set-up costs
    - running costs
    - health and safety

13. Employees
    - legalities
    - wages

14. Professional advice
    - solicitor/licensed conveyancer
    - accountant/bookkeeper
    - bank account
    - VAT and Inland Revenue
    - insurance
    - trade associations
    - training

CASHFLOW FORECAST

for a new business setting up in February

YEAR ONE	January	February	March	April	May	June	July	August	September	October	November	December	Totals
CASH INCOME		2000.00	3000.00	4000.00	5000.00	6000.00	7000.00	7000.00	6000.00	6500.00	7500.00	15000.00	69000.00
Cash Outflows:													
Stock		7000.00	4000.00	3000.00	2000.00	2500.00	3000.00	3500.00	3500.00	7000.00	4000.00	4000.00	43500.00
Rent				2276.56			2276.56			2276.56			6829.68
Business Rates		179.11	179.11	186.28	186.28	186.28	186.28	186.28	186.28	186.28	186.28	186.28	2034.74
Electric		20.00		100.00			100.00			100.00			320.00
Phone		20.00		60.00			60.00			60.00			200.00
Service Charge				175.00			175.00			175.00			525.00
Contents Insurance		100.00	100.00	100.00	100.00	100.00	100.00	100.00	100.00	100.00	100.00	100.00	1100.00
Stationery		10.00	10.00	10.00	10.00	10.00	10.00	10.00	10.00	10.00	10.00	10.00	110.00
Petrol		65.00	65.00	65.00	65.00	65.00	65.00	65.00	65.00	65.00	65.00	65.00	715.00
National Insurance			26.00			26.00			26.00			26.00	104.00
Accountant													0.00
Legal Costs		600.00											600.00
Shop Fitting		500.00											500.00
Personal Drawings					1000.00	1500.00	1500.00	1500.00	1500.00	1500.00	1500.00	1500.00	11500.00
TOTAL OUT		8494.11	4380.11	5972.84	3361.28	4387.28	7472.84	5361.28	5387.28	11472.84	5861.28	5887.28	68038.42
NET FLOW		-6494.11	-1380.11	-1972.84	1638.72	1612.72	-472.84	1638.72	612.72	-4972.84	1638.72	9112.72	961.58
CASH AT START OF MONTH		10000.00	3505.89	2125.78	152.94	1791.66	3404.38	2931.54	4570.26	5182.98	210.14	1848.86	
CASH AT END OF MONTH		3505.89	2125.78	152.94	1791.66	3404.38	2931.54	4570.26	5182.98	210.14	1848.86	10961.58	

No drawings will be made for the first three months as I have sufficient personal funds set aside.

Rateable value assumes 4% increase this year

Petrol assumes one trip to wholesalers per week

Figures in italics are estimated

Rent allows for two months rent free period as per lease

WEEKLY EXPENDITURE RECORD

Week No: Week Commencing:

PAYMENTS FOR STOCK

DATE/ CHEQUE No.	PAYEE	CASH AMOUNT	CHEQUE AMOUNT	CREDIT CARD AMOUNT

PAYMENTS OTHER THAN FOR STOCK	CASH AMOUNT	CHEQUE NUMBER	CHEQUE AMOUNT	DIRECT DEBIT/ STANDING ORDER
NATURE OF PAYMENT				
Employee costs				
◆ Wages				
◆ PAYE and NIC				
Premises costs				
◆ Rent and Rates				
◆ Heating and Lighting				
◆ Insurance				
◆ Cleaning				
Renewals and repairs				
General administration				
◆ Telephone				
◆ Postage and carriage				
◆ Stationery				
Motor expenses				
◆ Fuel				
◆ Service and repair				
Travel and subsistence				
Advertising and entertainment				
Legal and professional				
Banking charges				
◆ Current account				
◆ Merchant services				
Security				
Fire servicing				
VAT				

Key
PAYE and NIC   = Pay As You Earn and National Insurance contributions paid by employer for employees
Renewals and repairs = all maintenance costs which do not have their own heading

BANK ACCOUNT RECONCILIATION SHEET

NARRATIVE	DEBITS	CREDITS	BALANCE
Opening balance 1 January			Nil
Cash credit 7 January (week 1 takings)		£500.00	£500.00
Cheque no 1	£20.00		£480.00
January insurance direct debit	£50.00		£430.00
Cash credit 13 January (week 2 takings)		£700.00	£1130.00
Cheque credit " " " "		£50.00	£1180.00
Credit card credit " " " "		£250.00	£1430.00
Cheque no 2	£500.00		£930.00
Cheque no 3	£200.00		£730.00
January bank charges	£5.00		£725.00

SAMPLE LETTER REQUESTING REFERENCES

Dear Sirs

Re: Miss A B L Helper

The above named has applied to me for the position of Retail Sales Assistant and given your name as a referee.

I understand that you employed Miss Helper as a Sales Assistant in the Toy Department from June 1999 until November 2001 and as a Supervisor in the Giftware Department from November 2001 until March 2004. Please confirm that this is the case, and advise as to whether in your opinion she performed her tasks competently and conscientiously.

I would be grateful if you could confirm whether or not you consider Miss Helper to be an honest, reliable and responsible employee, and let me know her reasons for leaving and her sickness record.

Your reply will be treated in the strictest confidence.

Yours faithfully

....

Proprietor

Enc: stamped addressed envelope

STAFF INDUCTION SHEET

Name: ....   **Start Date:** ....

Introductions to other members of staff
Full time staff: Ann Andrews, Bill Benson
Saturday staff: Carol Collins, Danny Devlin

Shop opening hours
9.30–5.30 Monday to Friday
9.00–5.30 Saturday
10.30–4.30 Sunday (April to December)
Need to arrive 15 minutes before opening time to vacuum the floor, put
float in till, and prepare shop for opening on time.

Contact telephone numbers
Shop   01234 567890
Owner   01987 654321   (home)   07912 345678 (mobile)

Health and safety
Location of: toilet
                    fire extinguishers, alarm and drill
                    rubbish

Serving customers
Using the till and credit card machines
Accepting cheques
Giving receipts
Giving refunds and exchanges
Wrapping up the sale: bags and boxes

Security
Staff vigilance
Shop alarm
What to do about breakages
Shop intercom and video recordings

Re-stocking and product knowledge
Clothes
Cosmetics
Jewellery
Smoking paraphernalia – do not sell to under 16s
Sunglasses

Cleaning
Vacuum cleaning – shop, changing rooms, windows
Dusting – shelves, products, counters
Glass cabinets and mirrors
Stock

Staff handbook

USEFUL CONTACTS

Trade shows

www.exhibitions.co.uk provides a comprehensive listing of all consumer, public, industrial and trade exhibitions to be held in major venues around the UK. Search by exhibition type, date, organiser or venue.

UK travel information

www.visitbritain.com/vb3-en-gb/ gives accommodation, transport and practical advice.

South Warwickshire Tourism
Tel: 01789 415061

Stratford-upon-Avon Tourist Information Office
Tel: 01926 884666

Harrogate Tourist Information Office
Tel: 01423 537300

Shop fitting and supplies

See *Yellow Pages*:
Shop fitting suppliers
Display fittings and fixtures
Paper bags and sacks.

www.morplan.com   Tel: 0800 451122
www.ikea.co.uk
www.diy.com (B&Q)

Trade associations, directories and publications

There are no end of associations, directories and other publications, whatever your particular line of business. Publications include:

The Retail Buyer
Retail Week
Market Trader & Independent Retailer
The Trader

Search the Internet and ask your newsagent. Once you are on the trade exhibition mailing lists you will be inundated with information.

Importing
Flights and accommodation
Trailfinders, Bristol Office
Tel: 0117 929 9000

Rum Jungle Hotel, Kuta, Bali
email: rjungle@indosat.net.id

Cargo
www.azfreight.com lists agents, brokers, couriers, airlines and airports; all the contacts you could ever need for worldwide airfreight.

www.wtxglobal.com/glossary/ gives an explanation of the technical terms used in the cargo industry.

Khrisna Bali International Cargo
email: kbcline@indosat.net.id

Courier services
United Parcel Service
www.ups.com

TNT
www.tnt.com

Maps and guidebooks
Lonely Planet produce in-depth guidebooks, maps and phrasebooks for virtually anywhere you want to travel to. The guidebooks provide background information about the country as well as information on where to stay, how to travel around and places to visit.   www.lonelyplanet.com

Nancy Chandler produces an annually updated map of Bangkok. It is a hand-drawn map which includes details of local markets and the goods they sell. It is available at most English-language bookshops in Bangkok.

Expediter services (customs clearance)
Gatwick Expediter Management Services Ltd
Tel: 01293 567643
www.gem-s.com

Government advice

The No Nonsense Guide to Government Rules and Regulations for Setting Up Your Business is available from your local office:

Business Link
Tel: 0845 600 9 006
www.businesslink.org

Welsh Development Agency National Gateway
08457 969798
www.wda.co.uk

Invest Northern Ireland
Tel: 028 9023 9090
www.investni.com

Small Business Gateway (Scotland)
Tel: 0845 609 6611
www.sbgateway.com

Highlands and Islands Enterprise
Tel: 01463 234171
www.hie.co.uk

The booklet *Business Leases and Security of Tenure* is available from:
Department of the Environment
Publications Store
Building No 3, Victoria Road
South Ruislip, Middlesex

Department of Trade and Industry
www.dti.gov.uk

Import Licensing Branch
Tel: 01642 364333/334   for *A Guide to Import Licensing*
Tel: 01642 553671   to confirm if an import licence is required.

HM Customs & Excise
www.hmce.gov.uk

Music licensing

Performing Rights Society   Phonographic Performance Ltd
29 Berners Street   1 Upper James Street
London   London
W1 4AA   W1F 9DE
Tel: 020 7 580 5544

Licences are required from both these organisations to play recorded music in public (CDs, tapes or records). Only the Performing Rights Society licence is required if playing background music from a radio or television.

Professional photographer

www.mep-photography.co.uk

REFERENCES

<u>Staffing</u> (Chapter Seven)

Belbin, RMN (1981) *Management Teams: why they succeed or fail.* London, Heinemann.

Herzberg, F, Mausner, B and Snyderman, BB (1959), *The Motivation to Work*, 2nd edition, John Wiley.

<u>Up and Running</u> (Chapter Four)

Bruner, G (1990) 'Music, Mood and Marketing', *Journal of Marketing*, October, pp94–104.

Cockerton, T, Moore, S and Norman, D (1997) *Cognitive test performance and background music*

Michael Morrison, Monash University, 'The power of music and its influence on international retail brands and shopper behaviour: a multi case study approach.' (soundtherapy.co.uk).

THE STATISTICS

◆ Around 500,000 people set up in business every year. 68% do so for the first time.

◆ It takes an average of 13 weeks from making the decision to take the plunge until the point where the business starts trading.

◆ The average cost of setting up in business is £17,680, of which 44% is spent on equipment, 29% on premises and 9% on stock. (Shops need very little equipment so in my experience the cost of setting up is much lower.)

◆ The average turnover for a small business in its first year is £100,000. (This is only the average. In general, the harder you work the greater the possibilities to make the sky the limit.)

◆ 63% of small business owners agree that running a business is stressful, but 90% of them do not regret setting up in business.

◆ New small business owners work an average of 51.5 hours per week and take an average of five days' holiday in the first year. (If this is not for you then now is the time to say!)

◆ Half of new businesses are likely to cease trading within three years of formation.

◆ There were over 3.7 million small business enterprises in the UK at the start of 2002. These businesses accounted for more than half of the UK's business turnover and employment.

◆ Research in October 2003 indicated that 3.5% of the adult population in Great Britain were in the process of starting their own business. A further 0.6% were starting a business on behalf of their employer.

◆ More people were starting a business in Torbay than anywhere else in England, in the third quarter of 2003.

◆ The first half of 2004 saw the highest level of business start-ups since tracking began in 1988.

◆ A small business enterprise is defined as having between 0 and 49 employees. A micro business has fewer than 10 employees.

Statistics courtesy of Barclays Bank plc and the Department of Trade and Industry.

INDEX

If you want to know how ... to start your own business

'The road you live in, the bakery you stop at to get your morning coffee and pastry, the pub you frequent; none of it would be there if someone hadn't dreamed about it first. This workbook aims to help you shape your dreams of running your own business into rock-solid reality, acting as a guide for each step of the way.'

Cheryl D. Rickman

The Small Business Start-up Workbook

A step-by-step guide to starting the business you've dreamed of

Cheryl D. Rickman

An up-to-date approach to self-employment and business start-up, this workbook shows you how to research your business idea, plan the right marketing strategies and manage effective teams. It offers a selection of:

- real-life case studies
- practical exercises
- checklists
- worksheets

Other well-known entrepreneurs reveal what would have done differently, what their biggest mistakes have been and what they've learnt: Dame Anita Roddick, Julie Meyer, Stelios Haji-Ioannou, Simon Woodroffe and others expose their best and worst decisions and contribute their tips for succeeding in business.

ISBN 1 84528 038 5

If you want to know how … to use your business to fund your pension

'Providing for your retirement has never been so urgent a topic as it is now. At the time of writing this book, there has barely been a week go by without some item in the newspapers relating to pensions in some form or other. I hope this book will serve as a wake-up call to those who are tempted to put off providing for their retirement.'

John Whiteley

Your Business, Your Pension

How to use your business to provide for a better retirement

John Whiteley

If you are self-employed or are starting your own business you need to think about how you are going to fund your pension. This book outlines the basis of the State pension provision, then goes on to detail the various ways you can use your business to provide for your retirement.

- Make use of the generous tax advantages provided by the Inland Revenue
- Understand the regulatory framework of providing a pension for yourself and your employees
- Learn about SIPPs, SSASs UURBS, FURBS and all the other pension devices
- Gain information on how to sell a business or pass it on to your family

ISBN 1 84528 042 3

If you want to know how ... to do your own book-keeping and accounting

'In "doing the books" you will be at the very heart of the business, with your hands on the controls. You will be involved in the management of its assets and liabilities, its expenses and its profit margins.'

Peter Taylor

Book-keeping & Accounting for the Small Business

How to keep the books and maintain financial control over your business

Peter Taylor

'A guide to accounting procedures for sole traders, partnerships and limited companies... includes real life examples' – The Times

'Compulsory reading for those starting a new business and for those already in the early stages.' – Manager, National Westminster Bank (Midlands)

'An easy-to-understand manual on double-entry book-keeping that anyone can follow.' – Business First

ISBN 1 85703 878 9

If you want to know how ... to start and run your own business

'Running your own business can be a very rewarding and fulfilling experience, but there are no secret tricks to being successful... Success will only come through hard work and through always offering something that the consumer wants, at the right price, in the right place, and in the right quantity. This book covers all the essential points you need to know and think about before you actually go ahead and start your own business.'

Alan Le Marinel

Start and Run Your Own Business

The complete guide to setting up and managing a small business

Alan Le Marinel

Whether you dream of owning a corner shop or starting the next High Street chain, there are few more exciting prospects than starting your own business. This book will guide you through the whole start up process and steer you on towards success. It will help with:

- Defining your business strategy
- Researching the market and setting the right price
- Writing a business plan and raising finance
- Recruiting and managing staff
- Forecasting, budgeting and accounting
- Buying an existing business or franchise

Recommended by the Sunday Times – Business

ISBN 1 85703 988 2

If you want to know how ... to run a successful small business

'Running a business is never easy. More often than not it's a roller-coaster ride through a range of hazards and difficulties. But one thing is for sure: life will rarely, if ever, be dull. This book has one single purpose – to help you build a better business.'

Neil Bromage

100 Ways to Make Your Business a Success

A resource book for small businesses

Neil Bromage

'Avoid those pitfalls and hit big time.' – Sunday Mail

'No waffle, no preaching, just straightforward advice written in an unfussy, no bulls..t manner. What a nice change.' – K. Trimble, Gaelkat Ltd

'The book is a valuable source of factual information that can be utilised in local and nationwide businesses.'– The Gazette

ISBN 1 84528 017 2

How To Books are available through all good bookshops, or you can order direct from us through Grantham Book Services.

Tel: +44 (0)1476 541080

Fax: +44 (0)1476 541061

Email: *orders@gbs.tbs-ltd.co.uk*

Or via our website

www.howtobooks.co.uk

To order via any of these methods please quote the title(s) of the book(s) and your credit card number together with its expiry date.

For further information about our books and catalogue, please contact:

How To Books
3 Newtec Place
Magdalen Road
Oxford OX4 1RE

Visit our web site at

www.howtobooks.co.uk

Or you can contact us by email at info@howtobooks.co.uk